Cheshire Cats

A play

Gail Young

Samuel French — London
www.samuelfrench-london.co.uk

Please see page iv for further copyright information.

CHESHIRE CATS

First performed by Guilden Sutton Players at Guilden Sutton village hall in November 2005, and subsequently performed at the Edinburgh Fringe in August 2006 and the Gateway Theatre, Chester, November 2006. Performed in the published ensemble format at the Forum Studio Theatre Chester by Tip Top Productions, April 2011, with the following cast of characters:

Vicky	Gwen Cowan
Maggie	Emma Careless
Hilary	Pippa Redmayne
Siobhan	Alison Pritchard
Yvonne	Tiz Corcoran
Andrew	Richard Cannon
Aerobics Instructor	Jessica Martin
Ron	Martin Fraser
Madge	Maureen Shakeshaft
Handsome Drunk	Richard Taylor
Policeman	Richard Taylor
Radio Voice	Eric Jones
Station Announcer	Simon Johnson
Marshalls	Eric Jones, Dave Pearce, Olivia Gough, Fiona Paterson

Directed by Gail Young
Produced by Sarah Green

CHARACTERS

Hilary, bombastic, middle-aged team leader/
        organizer.

Siobhan, caring and diplomatic. Old friend of Hilary.

Yvonne, overworked/overweight stressed-out mum
        and friend of Hilary.

Maggie, overweight younger mum.

Vicky, artistic, fit, glamorous middle-aged divorcee

Andrew, trim toyboy.

Aerobics Instructor, may be played by person
        playing Andrew in the version of the play
        for 6 characters.

Handsome Drunk, may be played by person playing
        Andrew in the version of the play for
        6 characters.

Madge, elderly cockney marshall, can double up
        with the person playing Siobhan or Hilary
        in the version of the play for 6 characters.

Ethel, elderly cockney marshall, can double up
        with the person playing Siobhan or Hilary
        in the version of the play for 6 characters.

Additional characters for the ensemble version of the play:

Policeman, can double with **Handsome Drunk** if
        required.

Ron, elderly cockney marshall, married to Madge.

Marshalls, between 2 and 5 needed.

Photographers, at least 2 needed, preferably male.

Radio Voice

SYNOPSIS OF SCENES

ACT I   Training: a park.

ACT II Travelling: Chester train station/a train.

ACT III Walking: London.

ACT IV Returning: Chester train station.

Time — the present

INTRODUCTION

Grown women, aching feet and heaving bosoms! Follow the girls' emotional journey as they aim to speedwalk their way to fundraising success in the London Moonwalk while also enjoying a girly weekend away in the capital. Trainers and wildly decorated bras are in, high heels and designer labels out — but a last minute substitute to the team doesn't meet the physical criteria! This play is a comic tribute to all those who participate in and marshall the Moonwalk and other charity walking events everywhere. As so many people nowadays participate in such events worldwide, audiences identify very quickly with both the story and the characters.

The play has been successfully staged with minimal setting and props in both small village halls and much larger venues. It was originally written and performed as an ensemble piece for 11 people, but to accommodate smaller casts, and to allow for the financial constraints that often face professional theatrical productions, the script has been revised so that it can be performed either as an ensemble piece or with a cast of just 6 with some doubling and trebling of parts. To accommodate both cast sizes there are two versions of Act III in the script. I love the ensemble version as it is more fun for all!

The original title of "Cheshire Cats" echoed the name of the walking team in the script, and I directed and acted alongside fellow members of Guilden Sutton Players in the very first performances in Guilden Sutton Village Hall (near Chester) in November 2005. The Players were a fundraising tour de force, and we took it to the Edinburgh Fringe in August 2006 to raise funds for Walk the Walk and to support their launch of the Edinburgh Moonwalk that summer. The play was a "Fringe Sell Out Show 2006" with Claire Black reviewing it in *The Scotsman*, stating that "this is a genuinely funny and even touching ensemble piece".

To date all performing groups have admirably raised considerable funds to donate to a cancer-related charity or hospice of their choice. My sincere hope is that this charitable approach will continue in all future productions. I know that you will have a lot of fun with the play.

Break a leg,

Gail Young

For more information visit www.cheshirecats.org.uk

ACT I — TRAINING

A rural area

The only items on stage are four pink chairs representing a park bench set centrally. Traffic noise in the background and birdsong can be heard

The Lights come up on Maggie and Vicky jogging gently on the spot and performing stretching exercises. Vicky is dressed to kill in tight sporting Lycra; Maggie is dressed in a baggy t-shirt and tracky bottoms to hide her bulges

Vicky (*exercising confidently and expansively as she talks*) The others should be here soon, Maggie. They did promise firmly that they would be here at this time. Ten a.m., Hilary said. The last time I met them here I arrived — (*pointing to her watch*) — on the dot, and had to put up with truck drivers whistling at me ... (*She stops as she fondly remembers the attention*) ... Amongst other things ... (*She resumes exercising*) ... while I was warming up for half an hour, while waiting for them all to arrive.

Maggie (*tentatively copying Vicky's stretching exercises*) I was so pleased when your sister Chloe rang and asked me if I wanted to be in the team, Vicky. I told her how much I want to lose weight since I've had the baby! I thought she would be here today — is everything all right with her little one?

Vicky Teething problems with the baby, that's all — she'll be at the next practice walk so don't worry. Anyway — I'll look after you today ...

Maggie I don't think I've ever been in a team for anything, you know. Sport was never my strong subject at school... (*She laughs nervously*)

Vicky (*carrying on with a variety of seductive-looking stretching exercises*) Well — I knew you wanted to get into better shape — and with this you can get fit, lose weight — and raise money for a good cause at the same time. Are you still going to the Pilates classes at the leisure centre?

Maggie (*still copying Vicky and exercising as best she can*) Not so much now ... it all got a bit confusing. What with all that clenching your buttocks and concentrating on your front, middle and back bottoms, I just couldn't get my head round it half the time, never mind me muscles ... I mean to say — the things you were asked to clench. I found it all a bit distracting. And it was difficult to keep it up at home with the kids jumping all over me while I was in the middle of a pelvic floor exercise ...

Vicky Well — never mind that now — forget all that clenching and get stretching! The stretching is very important, you know. It doesn't matter how fit you are, if you don't warm up properly then you can really have problems later in the walk. Now come on, I haven't seen you stretch your spine yet. (*She demonstrates as she talks Maggie through the exercise*) Bend down ever so slowly — stretching those finger tips all the way down, just touch your toes, and then come up very slowly. Just try and stretch your back a little bit — loosen up your spine.

Maggie (*on her way slowly down*) I do tend to find this difficult, you know. I suffer terribly from a bad back since I've had the baby. I know the walking helps it, but ... It can just go, you know — just like that ... (*Her head reaches her knees*)

Vicky lowers her head to her own knees for the second time

Vicky (*looking across at Maggie*) Really? You'd never know.
Maggie (*with her head still down; solemnly*) Thank you.
Vicky Now come up slowly. (*She straightens up like a trained dancer*)

Maggie remains static with her head between her knees

Well, perhaps not that slowly.

Pause. Maggie does not move

You can straighten up a bit faster, you know ...
Maggie I would if I could ... (*She stays down — her back has gone*)
Vicky Don't tell me ...
Maggie (*with her head still down*) Yes — just like that.
Vicky Oh dear — let me help you straighten up ...

She helps Maggie to straighten her back up. The back clicks into place

Maggie Aaah, that's better ...
Vicky (*speed-walking around with an exaggerated technique to encourage Maggie to move*) Just walk around a bit. That's it ... Get your arms moving ... that's right.

Maggie follows with a less than impressive technique. Vicky stops and observes

Now — there's a definite technique to how you should use your arms when you're speed-walking, you know. It's all to do with the blood flow. It stops your fingers getting fat while you walk ...

Maggie (*with a nervous laugh that should become a behavioural tic when she is nervous*) Sounds good to me — slim fingers to start with and then hopefully the rest of me will follow suit ...

Vicky Tell you what — we'll have a little practice at speed-walking before the others get here. Just copy me — you'll soon get the hang of it — a good pace — here we go.

Vicky carries on briskly demonstrating the speed-walking technique. Maggie struggles behind her to both keep up and master the technique. Vicky is unaware of this

Maggie (*walking, talking, and struggling for breath*) I'll be fine on the walk. Honestly. Walking is fine. It's just when I have to bend down or sit for a long time. I must admit I am a bit nervous, though, thirteen miles is a long way — you know — walking the equivalent of half a marathon. It's not something I do every day! (*She gives a nervous laugh that turns into a struggle for breath*)

Vicky (*speed-walking*) Neither do I! But it's all in a good cause, all for charity isn't it? We'll all stick together on the night, you'll see. And look on the bright side. We're only doing the half marathon in London. A lot of people do the full one — I just don't know how they manage it.

Maggie (*very out of breath now but still gamely following Vicky*) I'm just a bit concerned that I won't keep up with the team, that's all. After all, London is a big place isn't it? I'm just afraid I'll get left behind on the embankment. (*Laughing nervously*) I don't mind walking the streets for charity, but if I get left behind some folk might think I'm walking them for some other reason ... (*She gives an exhausted attempt to laugh again as she collapses in a heap on the bench, completely shattered by the warm up*)

Vicky (*stopping*) Look — it's not a race — it's a walk for charity. It doesn't matter how long the team takes as long as we all finish. That's what our team is all about, looking after each other, all pulling together.

Maggie (*standing*) Thanks, Vicky ... I'm really looking forward to meeting all the others now. You're right, we'll be just one big team all pulling together. Oh, it's going to be great. Really fun ... (*She* *starts to laugh but visibly jumps as she hears Hilary's voice bellowing offstage)*

Hilary (*off; shouting*) COME ON, SIOBHAN, FOR GOD'S SAKE KEEP UP WILL YOU, IT'S IMPORTANT WE ——

Hilary strides into view at this point, not noticing Vicky and Maggie

—— *ALL* KEEP ON TARGET, YOU KNOW. REMEMBER. I'M THE PACEMAKER FOR THIS TEAM AND I DON'T WANT ANY STRAGGLERS! WE'RE NOT IN THIS JUST FOR FUN, WE'RE IN IT TO WIN!

Hilary turns and strides to Vicky, checking her own watch as she does so. The constant checking of her watch for her walking speed is a behavioural tic of Hilary's

Hi, Vicky, sorry we're a little later than promised but we decided to walk to the meeting point today rather than drive — an extra couple of miles a day at this stage of the game really helps to reduce those overall minutes per mile.

Vicky (*diplomatically*) Hi, Hilary. This is Maggie — remember? Replacing Veronica in the team …

Hilary enthusiastically turns to Maggie, firmly shakes her hand, very jolly hockey sticks

Hilary Oh, Maggie. It's great to meet you at last. Vicky said you'd agreed to be in the team when Veronica dropped out due to gout. It is so good of you to fill in for her at this late stage of the training. You know Vicky's sister Chloe don't you? She said you might be interested.

Maggie (*timidly*) Yes, that's right. We've kept in touch since we had our babies.

Hilary (*proudly*) Well, I'm Hilary, Team Organizer. (*She smiles at Maggie, suddenly checks her watch, lets go of Maggie's hand abruptly, and marches to shout off stage again*) GET A BLOODY MOVE ON! I KNOW IT'S UPHILL BUT COME ON, WILL YOU!

Siobhan enters at a good walking pace, with an excellent speed-walking technique, but sweaty and out of breath

Siobhan (*collapsing on the bench*) I'm here, I'm here. You can stop bellowing now.

Vicky Hilary! Calm down. You sound like a flaming sergeant major. I know you're the team organizer but for goodness' sake, tone it down a bit will you?

Siobhan The pace is a bit quick today, I'm knackered already.

Hilary Oh all right, all right, less of the whingeing. Oh, by the way, Siobhan, have you met Maggie? She's a friend of Chloe's, and she's kindly agreed to take Veronica's place in the team.

Maggie shyly waves to Siobhan

Siobhan (*waving, exhausted*) Hello there, Maggie. Glad you could make it.

There is a quick mental head count by Hilary and she interrupts Siobhan

Hilary Hold on, hold on ... we're one short. Where's Yvonne? I thought she was behind you, Siobhan.

Siobhan So did I. Mind you, it was all a bit of a blur because I was marching that bloody fast to keep up with you.

Vicky, Siobhan and Maggie all go and look off stage into the distance for Yvonne

Vicky Can you see her?

Maggie God, where do you think she's got to?

Siobhan I think she must have turned right when I turned left at the crossroads. She's never had a strong sense of direction.

Hilary is visibly impatient as the girls continue to look for Yvonne

Siobhan (*gently calling*) Yvonne, Yvonne!

Vicky I'm a bit worried about her. These country lanes can be really lonely.

Maggie I know, I know.

Siobhan Do you think we should go back to that last T-junction, Hilary?

Vicky (*louder*) Yvonne, Yvonne.

Vicky
Siobhan } (*slightly louder; together*) Yvonne, Yvonne ...
Maggie

Hilary (*bellowing*) YVONNE ... YVONNE!

The others wince at the volume

Yvonne limps on unnoticed from the opposite side of the stage. She sits down on the bench and gingerly takes off her shoe and sock on her foot. She has a blister on her heel. She calmly observes the others shouting for her

Siobhan ⎫
Maggie   ⎬ (*together*) Yvonne, Yvonne ...
Vicky   ⎭
Hilary YVONNE. YVONNE!
Siobhan We might have to shout a little bit louder. She could be some way away ——
Hilary (*interrupting and deafening Siobhan*) YVONNE! Oh for Christ's sake, she must be able to bloody well hear us.
Yvonne (*calmly interrupting*) All right, all right! I can bloody well hear you. So much for walking round some (*quoting Hilary*) "quiet country lanes". (*She examines the blister, wincing*) My heel is absolutely killing me ...

All except Hilary are relieved to see Yvonne, and gather round her clucking like mother hens

Siobhan (*chief mother hen, sitting alongside Yvonne on the bench*) You poor thing. Now come on, Yvonne, let's have a look at that. My God, look at the size of the blister! How long has that been hurting you? That's right, hold your foot right up so I can see the damage.
Vicky That does look ever so sore.
Yvonne It is.

Hilary looks impatient, and she checks her watch yet again

Siobhan You should have shouted up that you had a blister and couldn't keep up. We're all in this together, remember. We're a team.
Maggie Blisters. Ugh! They can be really nasty can't they?
Vicky (*dramatically*) Do you know, I can remember the last time I had a blister. I wore new shoes for a day out at the races — killer heels! I was on my feet the whole time, and I was absolutely crucified by the end of the day by an awful blister just like that one.
Siobhan Has anyone got any plasters with them at all?
Maggie (*eager to please her new companions*) Yes, I've got some in my bum bag — hang on — just let me get them out for you. I thought

I'd be the one getting a blister today. (*Laughing nervously*) What size do you need? (*She produces an astonishing array of plasters of differing sizes from her bumbag*) We haven't met have we, Yvonne? My name's Maggie, I'm a friend of Chloe's, Vicky's sister. I'm new to the team.

Vicky She's taking Veronica's place.

Yvonne Oh yes, that's right. Well, it's nice to meet you, Maggie, and thanks for coming so well prepared today. I've never seen so many plasters.

Yvonne selects the biggest plaster and hands it to Siobhan

That one will do nicely.

Siobhan It looks miles too big.

Yvonne It's not for me, you fool, just do me a favour and stick it over Hilary's big gob will you?

Maggie giggles nervously. Hilary glares at Yvonne. Siobhan diplomatically ignores Yvonne's request and solemnly assesses the size of the plasters by holding them up against Yvonne's heel

Siobhan Mmm, no, no. That's still too big.

The rest of the girls — except Hilary — echo Siobhan's assessment of the plasters by murmuring "too big, yes too big"

Nooooo, that's too small.

Again the others echo agreement "too small — yes — far too small"

(*Pleased*) Yes ... now that one looks just ——

Hilary (*loudly interrupting*) "Yes, that one looks just right!" It's like *Goldilocks and the Three Bears*. For God's sake, it is just a blister. She hasn't broken her foot or anything!

Vicky Oh, Hilary! You wouldn't like it if you had a blister like that, would you?

Siobhan applies the plaster to Yvonne's heel

Hilary No I would not, and neither did you, Vicky, when you wore your new shoes to the races did you? There is a price to be paid when you're breaking new shoes in, isn't there? (*She snatches up Yvonne's* *discarded trainer from the floor*) Because the problem with new shoes is that they do rub, and so do new trainers, don't they, Yvonne?

Hilary turns and stares pointedly at Yvonne, holding the new trainer aloft like a piece of evidence in a court case. Siobhan and Vicky gasp loudly as an unwritten law has been broken. Maggie looks confused

Yvonne Guilty as charged, me lud! I know we agreed that all new trainers must be broken in at least a month before the walk in London but my old ones are so naff, and I want to look good. I don't go to London every week, and I just want to look nice.

Yvonne looks to Hilary for forgiveness which is not forthcoming

It's not a crime is it?

Hilary No, it is not a crime, Yvonne, but it means we have incidents like this. (*She points to her watch*) We have now lost at least ten minutes, and we were aiming for a personal best today. But look on the bright side, at least it has happened today and not in London.

Hilary dismissively tosses the trainer to Yvonne. Yvonne scrabbles to catch it

Siobhan Yvonne, don't worry. I don't know about everyone else but I needed a breather just then.

Vicky Hilary, I think you're losing sight of the fact that this walk is about raising money for a breast cancer charity. I know it's a power walk, but it's the taking part and raising the money that is important, not how fast we walk.

Siobhan Vicky is right. The target should really be how much money we can raise as a team. It's been great that you've got us all so fit doing all these walks, but the real objective is to raise money.

Yvonne And it's a girlie weekend away in London for us all as well. A bit of fun. We agreed that when we decided to do it after doing the Race for Life and the Starlight walk last year. You said yourself that it would be good for us all to get away for a weekend. I know that it's nice to get some personal satisfaction from a fast time, but it's not the be-all and end-all is it? I just want to have a good time and look nice as well. I don't go to London every day ...

She runs out of steam and looks to the group for support. They all loudly agree and glare at Hilary accusingly

Hilary (*peeved*) All right, ladies. I've got the message, I have got the message! I know I'm only the group organizer. I know I'm only the one who has completed all the paperwork, booked the hotel in London, sorted out the team training programme and the train tickets ... but hey, what do I know? Obviously nothing!

She stomps away, turns her back on the others and folds her arms. The rest of the group exchange looks. There is an awkward silence. The rest of the group silently encourage Yvonne to mend the rift. Yvonne rises to her feet and limps to Hilary, still minus one shoe and sock

Yvonne (*soothingly*) Now come on, Hilary — don't get in a strop. This is all my fault, I just couldn't resist these trainers, and you have to admit — (*she holds the offending trainer up to Hilary's face*) — they are quite snazzy!
Hilary Well, considering they are new, they absolutely stink.
Yvonne (*sniffing the trainer*) Yes, they can pong a bit on a hot day, can't they?

Hilary shows no sign of softening. Yvonne looks anxiously back at the others who silently encourage her to persevere

Oh come on, Hilary, you know we all appreciate the effort you've put into this, we really do.

Yvonne raises her hand behind Hilary's back to encourage the others to verbally agree. The group loudly voice their agreement

Siobhan Of course we do.
Vicky We couldn't have managed all the training without you.

Hilary visibly relaxes momentarily

Yvonne But you can be a bit of a hard taskmaster sometimes.

Hilary's back stiffens and she folds her arms again. Yvonne looks furtively at the group for silent advice. Vicky mimes putting her arm round Siobhan, hugging her in a comradely manner and silently urges Yvonne to do the same to Hilary

(*Grasping Hilary round the shoulder as best she can*) Look, we have all got a lot further to walk today, and we need you to ... well ... show us the way, for starters. I've got a terrible sense of direction, and you are our team leader, aren't you? All groups need a leader and you're ours. After all — you told us all you were at the initial team meeting, didn't you?

Hilary nods in agreement. She is weakening now. The tension drops. She smiles at Yvonne

Great. Now come on, you explain the rest of the route for today while I put my trainer back on.

Hilary (*returning to leader mode*) Now, we have got another eight miles to walk today.

Yvonne winces and pauses at this thought as she limps back to the group

So, if that is going to be a problem for you, Yvonne, please say so now, and we will come up with another route for this morning.

Yvonne (*sitting back down on the bench to put on her shoe and sock again*) No. No. The plaster will help a lot, I know. Perhaps if I walk at a slightly slower pace with ... say ... Maggie, as she is new to the training?

Maggie (*thrilled to be asked to walk at a slower pace, nodding agreement vigorously and rushing to Yvonne's side*) Yes, yes, that's a great idea, Yvonne. A great idea. I don't think I could manage the full pace this morning. (*Laughing nervously*) A stroll to the paper shop is more my style normally. So, yes, yes, yes please Yvonne, that's fine with me. Wonderful. Absolutely fine! (*She laughs nervously*)

Vicky (*placing herself alongside Maggie*) I'll walk at Yvonne's pace as well, and give her a lift home afterwards when I drop Maggie off. So don't worry about us lot, Hilary, just tell me the rest of the route.

Hilary (*appeased*) OK, OK. Now, the route we are doing today is the same as we did on Tuesday morning. The circular route that ends up back here. Can you all remember that?

Siobhan Oh yes, I remember. The one that goes past those lovely new barn conversions, and then you turn right at the T-junction, and then left after the bridge over the canal? (*She is off on a tangent now, and chats away in a leisurely manner to the group*)

Hilary looks on

Do you know, those barns have such great kerb appeal. The landscaping is *soooo* inventive. And they are very reasonably priced, and beautifully finished inside. Lovely internal doors. The worktops are all granite in the kitchen, oak wood floors throughout, gorgeous bathrooms, and the landscaping is first class, really imaginative, beautiful decking and ——

All the group except Hilary are totally engrossed in this welcome diversion from speed walking and are murmuring interest

Hilary (*interrupting loudly*) Oh, for God's sake, Siobhan. Since you got that part-time job at that estate agent's your life is just a series of new property developments. Can we get back to the route, please? Yvonne. Have you got your mobile on you?

Yvonne Yes.

Hilary OK — so if you get lost again give me a buzz on mine straight away and I will redirect you.

Yvonne Fine, fine.

Hilary Right, folks, that sorts out the team split for this morning. So now it's time for the fun bit of the morning — the team strip!

Excited girly noises from the group. Vicky purposefully steps up alongside Hilary

We all know that Vicky came up with the idea for this outfit when the team name was agreed, so hopefully it's going to reflect the name ——

Siobhan (*interrupting Hilary's flow*) I bet it's good, Vicky, you're soooo creative.

Maggie Yes. That last art exhibition you staged at the village hall was absolutely fantastic. (*Bashfully*) When I went to see it with Chloe it inspired me to sign up for the Access Course in art that I'm doing now ...

Vicky (*touched by Maggie's admiration*) Really, Maggie? You never mentioned that before.

Maggie I know. (*Clasping her hands together and looking at Vicky adoringly*) Well, it's true. I'd really love to be an art teacher like you, it must be so satisfying.

Vicky Aaah, Maggie. (*She goes to Maggie and gives her a hug*) I feel really honoured that you've told me that. It's so sweet.

Hilary (*utterly exasperated at this further turn in the conversation, dragging Vicky away from Maggie*) For goodness' sake, can we have the mutual art appreciation session another time please! Right ... the team strip for the walk ... now girls, it is really important that we all wear the same outfit on the day as it will help us keep tabs on where

we are in the crowd. Remember this is a huge event — with masses of
other walkers, there will be thousands of them ...

*Vicky returns to Hilary's side to resume her role as model for the team
strip. The others sit like an appreciative audience*

You'll all remember that we wrote our suggestions for the team name
on a piece of paper and put it in a hat didn't we, ladies? And the name
that was drawn out was ...?

*Hilary looks towards the main group like a primary school teacher
expecting a group response*

All (*enthusiastically*) The Cheshire Cats!
Hilary Well done, girls. Very appropriate as we ——
Vicky (*interrupting Hilary*) As we're all dead catty!

The girls all laugh, except Hilary

Hilary (*in a matter-of-fact tone of voice*) Well, I was going to say as we
all live in Cheshire, but if the cap fits!

*Vicky is now bowing to the others in true luvvy style. There is good-natured
heckling from the others, e.g. "Can't wait to see it", "Get your baps
out", etc. Hilary is unimpressed and hushes them*

Vicky will try the team strip out today to make sure it is practical.

Group comments and noises start again

After all, we will be wearing it while walking a half marathon through
the streets of London, and it is really important that it's comfortable
and ...

*The rest of the group are now shouting encouraging but lewd remarks
to Vicky. Vicky is loving every minute and strutting centre stage like a
seasoned stripper*

(*Giving up trying to control the group at this point*) Oh, I give up. Here
for your approval is Vicky's design.

*The stripper theme tune plays with the group joining in. Vicky obliges by
doing a comic strip that ends in her taking the tracksuit top off to much
whooping and hollering. She also has a tail and ears in her bum bag and*

long slinky black gloves to add to the outfit and her bra has been dressed up to look like a cat's face — she is Catwoman personified. Siobhan jumps up and goes to Vicky to admire the costume. The others fall about laughing, except Hilary who sits stunned and bemused

Siobhan God, Vicky. That is *sooooo* cool, really feminine. You look fantastic — just like Catwoman!

Vicky Thanks, Siobhan. It's not expensive. I've bought enough of all the bits for everyone — so I thought we could have a girly night at my house and all bring our bras, and have a few glasses of wine while we have a joint sewing night. You know, a bit of a team bonding session.

Hilary (*standing up, looking horrified*) More like team bloody bondage you mean! We'll end up looking like a load of hookers if we wear that through the streets of London at midnight.

Siobhan Oh don't be such a flaming prude, Hilary. There will be loads of marshals and security guards along the route, and all the other teams will be wearing suggestive outfits as well. It is to raise cash for a breast cancer charity after all. My sex life could do with a bit of spicing up at the moment anyway. My hubby is away on business such a lot lately — if I get mistaken for a hooker I'll just consider it my lucky night.

Yvonne, Maggie, Siobhan and Vicky all chat. Hilary sits down and takes a local map from her bum bag, a small book, and a pen to check out the route and mileage for the day and to add it to her diary of walks

Yvonne I'll have to get scaffolding put in my bra — I'll need it welded together to look as good as Vicky ...

Maggie Do you know, I'll have to tone up my tummy muscles if we're wearing that on the night. I don't think I can get away with that outfit, folks — too much flab on show! (*She looks concerned*)

Vicky (*reassuringly*) Now don't worry — there's always a solution to disguising the flab. I'll give you a buzz to organize the group sewing night and we'll get it sorted.

Maggie (*appreciatively*) Thanks.

Siobhan (*still maternally checking Vicky's outfit over*) Now, are you sure that it won't chafe on the skin, Vicky? You are going to have to really check your boobs and your shoulders over at the end of this walk today to see whether or not those eyes and whiskers have rubbed on your skin or not.

Vicky I have used the softest of materials because of that, Siobhan, and ... (*She pauses dramatically, minces over to Hilary; in a suggestive tone of voice*) ... loads of Vaseline ... in all the right places.

Hilary (*looking up from her map of the area*) Oh shut up, will you. Bloody nymphomaniac ...

Vicky I wish.

Yvonne Vicky! You have become sex-mad since you got divorced.

Vicky Do you know, the truth is that I can't remember the last time I had sex, so all of my frustrated sexual tension has gone into *this*. (*She dramatically indicates her outfit*)

Yvonne Still no man on the scene then?

Vicky (*coyly*) No. Well, I say no, but I did meet a really nice guy recently.

Siobhan You sly thing not telling us! Where? Where? Come on, tell all!

Vicky At my little niece's christening of all things. He's an old school friend of Terry, my brother-in-law. It was a big event — Chloe and Terry's first baby and all that. And there he was.

Lighting changes to a pool of light on one side of the stage where Andrew will enter. The rest of the cast freeze. There is the sound of the christening party going on in the background

Andrew enters with two flutes of champagne

Vicky walks over to Andrew — still in her Catwoman outfit

Andrew Hi.

Vicky Hi.

Andrew Sorry I took so long to fetch you a drink. I've just been having my ear bent by Terry's mum. She hasn't seen me since Terry and I shared a house together at university, so we've just had a bit of a catch up. Time flies doesn't it?

Vicky Oh don't worry. Thanks for offering to fight your way to the drinks table for me.

She takes a glass from Andrew. They sip the champagne and there is a pause while they eye each other up

Andrew Chloe didn't tell me she had such a gorgeous older sister.

Vicky I'm not surprised. She never liked me meeting her men friends.

Andrew No?

Vicky No. Well, I had bigger boobs than her in our youth and she's never got over it really.

Andrew stares at Vicky's bust and hastily corrects his line of vision

Andrew Sorry.

Vicky For what?

Andrew Well, you know, now that you've mentioned it, I've gone and ... erm ... stared.

Vicky At what?

Andrew Your boobs, I mean cleavage — sorry — dress. Christ, I can't believe I've just said that! You'll have to forgive me. I'm out of practice, chatting up women. It's been a while. Sorry ... Well, I'd better go and mingle then. It's ... er ... been nice to meet you, Vicky. Apologies again for the boob — sorry, I mean gaffe ... yes, well ... perhaps we'll bump into each other again some time. (*He turns to go*)

Vicky When's that, then?

Andrew Pardon?

Vicky "Some time." If you're asking a girl out you'll have to be more specific than that.

Andrew Oh ... really? Yes ... you're right. I will. Well ... if it's OK with you I'll give you a buzz when I'm next in town.

Vicky I'll look forward to it. (*She hands him her empty glass*) In the meantime make yourself useful and get me a refill, will you. All this talk about my body has made me quite thirsty.

Andrew (*laughing*) Bossy little thing, aren't you? It's a good job that I like dominant women.

Andrew walks off

Vicky watches him go intently — she is still standing in the spotlight

Vicky (*turning to the audience she smiles and confides in them, speaking in verse*)

> He is sooo cute, a handsome guy!
> A bit too young? But tell me why
> Am I hung up about his youth?
> I think the time has finally come to face the truth
> And say I really *really* fancy younger men,
> And I don't want to be a flaming mother hen!
> But folk would talk ... and say I'm bad ...
> A naughty girl ... a little sad ...
> And all because I want a bit of fun
> With someone young enough to be my son!
> You know — an older man would really see no harm
> In having a young chick upon his arm
> A little minx, a bright young thing ...
> That really rings his ding-a-ling.

She thinks and then growls to herself seductively

> Equality for all, that's what I say,
> For I do feel the older man has had his day
> And younger men are sooo sublime —
> I actually think it's cougar time!
> Youths of today love older vamps,
> So I'll allow my inner tramp
> To surface at long last — in a *nice* way
> — and ask that buff young man if he can play
> A big cat game ... and if he's sure ...
> Well then we'll find a place where we can really roar!
> Equality for all, that's what I say,
> For I do feel the older man has had his day
> Why waste my time?
> I really really know it's cougar time!

She thinks to herself and growls

> And that young man is sooooooo sublime!
> This definitely is my cougar time!

She growls to herself

The Lights snap back up on the scene with the girls

Hilary (*loudly breaking the moment*) Talking of your sister, where is she today? This is the second training walk she's missed. She'll never be able to keep up with us all on the night ...

Siobhan Hilary, shut up will you? This is more important than a bloody walk! This could involve sex!

Hilary Well, as team organizer I need to know. Chloe's not dropping out like Veronica did is she?

Vicky (*indignantly*) No! She is just really busy with the baby at the moment that's all.

Yvonne Vicky, just ignore her. We need more information. Description?

Vicky Handsome ... charming in an awkward Hugh Grant sort of way ... sexy ...

Maggie Sounds good so far.

Yvonne Age?

Vicky A little bit younger than me.

Siobhan By how much?

Slight pause

Vicky Oh, it's not important ...
Siobhan ⎫
Yvonne ⎬ (*together*) Oooooooooh.
Maggie ⎭
Siobhan A toy boy!
Yvonne Doesn't that make you a cougar then?
Vicky I'm not answering that question.
Siobhan Why, what's the problem?
Vicky (*taking a deep breath before replying; sighing*) He's been married before.
Yvonne You fussy woman, so have you.
Vicky Yes, I know, but I don't really want to get involved with a guy who's got any baggage.
Siobhan Oh, get real, Vicky. He'd have to be a bloody monk! And if he hasn't got any baggage it just means that he's never had a life! Let's cut to the chase here. Did you give him your phone number?
Vicky Well ...
Siobhan ⎫
Yvonne ⎬ (*ad-libbing*) Oh come on, come on, spill the beans. (*Etc.*)
Maggie ⎭
Vicky Yes!
Siobhan ⎫
Yvonne ⎬ (*together*) Oooooh!
Maggie ⎭
Vicky Now stop it, I knew you would all behave like this if I told you.

Siobhan leads the others; chanting

Siobhan ⎫
Yvonne ⎬ (*together*) Name, name, name ...
Maggie ⎭
Vicky (*shouting petulantly*) No, I am not telling you. And anyway, he hasn't rung me yet. I've probably frightened him off.
Yvonne Oh come on, Vicky — this is really exciting. Your first possible date for twelve months!
Maggie You'll be like a teenager all over again.
Siobhan Candlelit dinners ...
Yvonne Canoodling in the car ...
Maggie Holding hands all the time ...

All including Hilary look wistfully into the distance, locked in their own little romantic fantasies

Hilary (*with a bored tone in her voice; starting to pack away her route map in her bum bag*) Finding out he picks his nose. (*Standing facing the group*) For goodness' sake, girls — can we get going again *please*! Just look at you, you're like a load of stupid teenagers. All your hearts should be pounding away now due to physical exercise, not fluttering away because of her menopausal sexual fantasies!

Siobhan Calm down, Hilary. And we're not all menopausal yet, you know. Just because Vicky's enjoying having a few hot flushes in anticipation of a hot date there's no need for that sort of attitude from you.

Hilary Oh come on, come on. We have GOT to get going again.

Vicky Yeah, come on folks. Hilary is right. I've got to give this outfit ... (*in a husky voice to annoy Hilary*) ... and all that Vaseline a good trial run. Now, can I just confirm that you are all happy to wear this?

Siobhan
Yvonne   } (*chorusing enthusiastically*) Yes!
Maggie

Hilary looks dubious. Vicky and the group look pointedly at her for her approval

Hilary Yeeeeeeahhh, all right then.
Vicky Great.

Yvonne and Maggie are still sitting on the bench. Vicky joins them and sits between them

Hilary (*facing them*) Right. I need to finish this walk in the best possible time. Yvonne? You, Vicky and Maggie just take your time. Siobhan and I will march on ahead if that's OK.
Yvonne Fine, fine. I've got your mobile number if we get lost.
Hilary Great. Just remember the barn development and all that tasteful landscaping and you'll be fine! Siobhan!

Siobhan assumes mock military mode and stands to attention. Hilary turns to face her

Siobhan (*saluting and shouting out like an American marine*) Yes, sir!
Hilary Very funny!
Siobhan All in the line of duty, sir!

Hilary joins in the charade. She turns on her heel in Sergeant Major mode alongside Siobhan. Both now face the audience

Hilary (*assuming a loud American Sergeant voice*) OK. Shoulders
   back, young lady. Are your leg muscles ready to take the strain?
Siobhan (*mock saluting — then shouting*) Yes, sir!
Hilary (*after a momentary silence, then she loudly and forcefully leads
   an American-style military marching chant*)
                    I don't know but I've been told.

*Vicky, Siobhan and Yvonne echo the lines in military unison as in all
good American military movies. They have all sung it many times before
on route marches with Hilary*

Vicky
Siobhan   } (*together*) I don't know but I've been told.
Yvonne
Hilary   London's streets are paved with gold.
Vicky
Siobhan   } (*together*) London's streets are paved with gold.
Yvonne

*Hilary starts to march on the spot. Siobhan copies her. Hilary continues
to chant*

Hilary   I don't know but it's been said.
Vicky
Siobhan   } (*together*) I don't know but it's been said.
Yvonne
Hilary   Cheshire Cats are good in bed.

Yvonne, Maggie and Vicky start giggling

Yvonne
Siobhan   } (*together*) Cheshire Cats are good in bed.
Vicky

*All the team chant together. Hilary starts to march off followed by
Siobhan*

All   Pump those muscles, hit your stride,
                     Makes you feel real good inside.
                     Hey ho, hey ho,
                     Here we go, here we go,
                     Not too fast, not too fast,
                     Not too slow, not too slow.

Hilary and Siobhan march off

Yvonne, Maggie and Vicky are left sitting on the bench. Yvonne and Vicky nod their heads and sing the words in unison as the chant fades out in the distance

Yvonne (*nosily turning to Vicky*) So. Any more info on this mystery man you've met then? Come on, dish the dirt.

Vicky What about him? I'm not giving you any more details, Yvonne. You can be so bloody critical about my men at times.

Yvonne No need to get all defensive. I'm really glad you're interested in someone again. I was beginning to think you'd become completely celibate!

Maggie Have you been off men since your divorce then, Vicky?

Vicky I wouldn't say that, but I have to confess that I'm a bit of a romantic really. I suppose I've just been waiting for Prince Charming to come along and sweep me off my feet. That hasn't worked, so I've decided to become a vamp instead.

Maggie Well, if this guy doesn't ring you, what was his name again?

Vicky Andrew ... hang on a minute ... I didn't tell you his name!

Yvonne Well done, Maggie, we got it at last!

Maggie If Andrew doesn't ring you then maybe you'll meet someone else when we're all away in London.

Yvonne (*very firmly*) No way! This is a "girls only" event. I am really looking forward to a man-free couple of days. No men to cook for, wash for, and clean for.

Vicky All right, all right. Keep your hair on. I've got the message. What's the matter with you anyway? I've always thought of you and your gang as Happy Families.

Yvonne More like snappy families at the moment! Look, I just want a really girly weekend away, that's all. I'm fed up of being the unpaid servant in our house. You should try dealing with a husband and three hulking great lads! They can be so flaming demanding at times. They don't know the meaning of the words "housework" or "cooking", and I've just about had enough of being tied to the kitchen sink.

Vicky I thought you had a dishwasher?

Yvonne I have, but you know what I mean! So I'm warning you, Vicky, no running off with any man at the weekend, even if it is Prince Charming.

Vicky OK, message received, but not all men are like that, you know.

Yvonne Well, you might be the incurable romantic, but I've yet to meet a bloke that treats me like a princess.

Vicky (*looking at her watch and jumping up as she sees the time*) Hey, come on girls — we'll have to make a move. It's time for the rear brigade to "hit their stride".

Maggie (*unenthusiastically*) Oh ... do we have to warm up again?

Vicky Forget that! I don't think we're going to be walking at double-quick pace now that *mein Führer* has left the camp!

Yvonne My calf muscles nearly caved in completely trying to keep up with Hilary on the way here. That woman is obsessed with speed walking. No wonder I got a blister. I don't think my heels have ever shifted so fast.

Maggie I must admit, I do feel a bit nervous now about being able to keep up with you all on the night, you know ... (*she laughs nervously*) ... now that I've met Hilary!

Vicky Oh, don't worry about her. As soon as we've gone a couple of miles in the Moonwalk in London, I'll definitely be slowing the pace down.

Yvonne So will I. It's not a race, it's all about raising money. You just stick with us and you'll be all right. And don't let Hilary's zealous streak frighten you, Maggie. If she hadn't taken all the time and trouble to organize this we probably wouldn't be doing it.

Vicky Yvonne's right. Her bark's worse than her bite. Anyway, come on you two. Time to let those leg muscles take the strain.

They all start pacing on the spot gently. Maggie again tentatively follows Vicky's lead

Blister recovered and at the ready, Yvonne?

Yvonne Yes, sir!

Vicky Spare plasters for our buddy's heel at the ready, Maggie?

Maggie In the bum bag, sir!

Vicky All together now.

Yvonne and Vicky chant in unison, with Maggie struggling to remember the words

All   I don't know but I've been told,
                      London's streets are paved with gold,
                      I don't know but it's been said,
                      Cheshire Cats are good in bed.
                      Pump those muscles, hit that stride.
                      Makes you feel real good inside.

Vicky strides off briskly, followed by Yvonne, limping

Maggie follows enthusiastically. Her back gives a definite twinge as the others leave the stage. She stops abruptly in her tracks and holds her back, singing the following line directly to the audience before she hobbles off

Maggie   I don't know but there's a risk,
                      I'm gonna slip a bloody disc ...

Maggie leaves

The Lights fade out

Sounds of a busy railway station immediately come up as the set is struck for Act II. They should include platform announcements/explanations for delayed trains etc. to and from Chester, from and to a variety of stations

ACT II

SCENE 1

A platform at Chester Railway Station

There should be two rows of four pink chairs set either side of the railway platform sign for "Chester". In the following scene these seats will double up as seats on the train

The Lights come up on Hilary and Siobhan already on the stage. They have a weekend bag each as well as their handbags etc. Hilary holds the train tickets for all the team in her hand. She is striding up and down anxiously checking her watch, drinking bottled water, and munching on an energy bar. Siobhan is sitting reading a magazine

Siobhan (*looking up; in a motherly tone*) Hilary — will you please stop pacing up and down like that, you'll be worn out before we get to London at this rate. Save your energy for tonight. The others will be here in a minute.

Hilary I've checked that information screen again and the good news is the train is due to arrive on time! No last-minute alterations or cancellations, thank God.

Siobhan (*languidly recalling*) Do you know, the last time I travelled by train it was an absolute nightmare. Stuck at Crewe for three hours. Christ, that was soooo depressing. Then I couldn't get a seat, and had to stand most of the way ... no refreshments on the train ... and the toilets were absolutely disgusting ...

Hilary Yes, yes ... That's enough, thank you — I get the picture.

A very long garbled platform announcement is heard, a male voice in a bored tone. Vital details about the London train fade in and out annoyingly. The girls listen intently

Announcer The train for London due to arrive at platform ... (*the announcer fades out or becomes garbled*) ... will now arrive at the revised time of ... (*fading out/becoming garbled again*). It will be calling at the following stations ... (*fading out/becoming garbled again*)

The next announcement is crystal clear

This is an urgent colleague announcement for John. An urgent colleague announcement for John ... Liverpool, two. United, one. I will repeat that, Liverpool, two. United, one.You owe me a tenner. I will repeat that, a tenner.

Siobhan (*philosophically*) Well, the important part of that announcement was about as clear as mud.

Hilary (*pacing up and down*) Where the hell are the others? I just cannot stand it when people arrive late. (*Holding up the tickets*) And I've got all the tickets and hotel information. I must have been off my proverbial trolley when I said I'd organize this weekend!

Siobhan Stop moaning, Hilary.

Hilary Why do I always volunteer for everything? (*She mimics herself*) "I'll get the tickets — I'll get the hotel organized ... I'll wipe your flaming bums for you."

Siobhan (*gently*) Because you bloody love it. Let's face it, you're an out-of-control control freak who loves nothing better than to organize everything and everybody. Why don't you delegate to people?

Hilary I've tried that, and all that happens is that I end up shouting at people even more because they haven't done things right. (*She pauses as she realizes Siobhan is right*) I know, I know. I've just got to trust people to get on with things themselves.

Siobhan Look, once you've dished out those train tickets to the girls just sit back and look after yourself for the rest of the weekend.

Hilary You're right. I could do with taking a back seat once we get there. Look at me! We haven't even started the walk yet and I'm absolutely frazzled already

Siobhan Come on, come and sit down by me till the others get here. You've got a long way to walk tonight, so rest your legs while you can.

Hilary sits by Siobhan. She manically leafs through her magazine, finishing it in double-quick time. Siobhan looks on. Slight pause

(*Tentatively*) How's your dad? I haven't seen him for ages. Did his big move go OK?

Hilary It went fine thanks.

Siobhan How's he doing in the new apartment?

Hilary He calls it a flat. He says apartments are American! You know what he's like. He's doing OK thanks, and actually he really loves it. I'm just so glad he's been positive about downsizing from the house. The garden was too much for him on his own, and really it was Mum who did the gardening so ... (*Her voice trails off momentarily as she thinks about her mum*) Anyway, he's really excited about us all doing the walk in London. At one stage he was talking about coming down with me and trying to spot us on the way round. I had to laugh to myself when he said that. I don't think he's got a clue how many people are taking part!

Siobhan Why don't you give him a buzz when we get to the hotel and let him know we've all arrived safely! He'll feel part of it then.

Hilary I will. (*Pause*) Between you and me I should ring him a lot more often than I do at the moment. I'm rubbish at that lately. I just feel like I need a bit of space now that we've got his flat and all the move sorted out. Mum's been gone nearly two years now, and all I seem to have been doing since then is run around and sort out one thing after another. It just all seems to have fallen on my shoulders because the rest of our family don't live locally. My dad's probably wondering what he's done wrong, but I just need a bit of time out ... a bit of time to myself ... some space ... normality ... (*Pause*) Oh, I don't know, Siobhan, sometimes I feel like I'm losing the plot ...

Siobhan No you're not. Come on now, your dad's great. He knows you've got your own life to lead as well as caring about him.

Hilary Yeah. You're right. He is great and I love him to bits. But things have changed. You know what me mum was like, always organizing family get-togethers, you know what I mean. She really took the time to keep us all in touch with each other, and now that she's gone we're all trying our hardest but — oh, I don't know — I sometimes feel it's slipping away — all that closeness ... I haven't stopped thinking about her all morning, you know, Siobhan. She loved going away with a gang of girls, and I just know that she'd have really enjoyed this weekend ... (*She is near to tears. She stands and moves away from Siobhan, embarrassed*) It's tough sometimes, I just miss her so much ... (*Pause; remembering, speaking in verse*)

> It's hard to see her face now in my mind,
> But easy to remember that she was so kind
> To everyone, not just her family —
> But we're the ones that miss her most of all, you see ...
> Her image fades a little every day,
> But still clear in my head are all the things
>   she'd say and do.
> Like when I'm really down and not so bright
> I feel her arms around me holding me so tight
> And I hear her saying "Come on love, listen to me —
> Life goes on you know, you'll see ... you'll see ..."
> I'm crying less with every passing day,

But it doesn't mean the longing's any less or gone away
I long for her to be with me right now
So that I can talk with her and tell her how
There's something really special in a mother's touch ...
I just miss her so much, so much ...
And every now and then I can still feel her eyes
            upon me as I go along my way
I just know she's looking out for me,
            but with every passing day
It's growing hard to see her face clear in my mind,
But easier to see that she was so very kind
To everyone, not just her family —
But we're the ones that miss her most of all you see ...
There's something really special in a mother's touch
And I just miss her so much, so very much ...

Siobhan moves to Hilary and puts her arm round her

Siobhan I know you do, we all do. You just have to remember that she'd be so proud of you doing this walk tonight in her memory. And your mum was a real party animal — she'd want you to really enjoy this weekend, you know she would. She loved a good laugh!

Hilary (*laughing through her tears*) You're right. She would. And she would have definitely been up for wearing a Catwoman outfit — even though she was a size eighteen!

They both laugh gently — then Hilary suddenly reverts to type

Mind you, talking of outfits, I just hope everyone has remembered everything. I was going to draw up a checklist for the team. It did cross my mind. It would be awful if someone forgot their bra or their trainers.

Siobhan We're all grown women, Hilary, we can organize ourselves, if you'd just give us the chance.

Hilary Yeah, you're right. And listen, thanks for being so supportive, Siobhan. I don't know what I would have done without you and the girls this last couple of years. (*She hugs Siobhan*)

Siobhan Now stop all that or you'll have me blubbing away next. (*She gently changes the subject and points up to the sky*) Hey, look at that. The sun's come out. It's a good sign. Your mum must be using her influence up there. Let's hope the weather stays good for tonight ...

Hilary The forecast is that it's going to be dry. We don't want any
rain do we? I don't fancy pounding the streets of London in soggy
trainers.

Yvonne (*off*) Yoo hoo, yoo hoo ...

*Yvonne bustles on with Maggie — both carrying their bags/magazines/
food for the train etc.*

Thank goodness we've found you two. We were nearly going to the
wrong platform and then we spotted you. God, those announcements
aren't very clear. (*Gleefully*) I am sooooooo excited. All girls together!
A real girly weekend away. No shirts to iron, no supermarket run, no
taxiing my lads around ...

*Yvonne and Maggie settle themselves and their belongings on the other
station bench*

Maggie (*to Yvonne*) And no men!

Yvonne Yes, no men! Not that I'm not happily married but there does
come a time, girls, when enough is enough. This is a bit of time out for
me, me pals ... (*adjusting her attributes*) ... and me boobs!

Maggie I can't remember the last time I went away with a gang of girls
for a weekend. (*She laughs nervously*)

Siobhan Me neither.

Yvonne Just a gang of girls, and up for a bit of fun ... How does that
song go — you know — (*She sings Cyndi Lauper's "Girls Just Wanna
Have Fun"*)

*Siobhan and Maggie join in with gusto for a few lines. Siobhan and
Yvonne carry on singing. Maggie talks over them to Hilary*

Maggie Hilary, I'm sorry we were a bit late getting here. (*She laughs
nervously*)

Hilary You're here now, don't worry about it ...

Maggie Still, all's well that ends well. I see you've got all the train
tickets. Are we all together?

Hilary goes to answer Maggie as she asks each question

Have you managed to check all the numbers yet? We have got reserved
seats haven't we?

Hilary (*making a decision to delegate; handing the tickets to Maggie*) Do
you know, Maggie, I haven't had a chance yet. Can you sort the tickets
out for me and allocate seats to everyone? Will you do that for me?

Maggie (*honoured*) Yes, yes of course, Hilary.

Maggie looks through the tickets as she sits down — showing off her allocated responsibilities to the others. Hilary returns to sit down by Siobhan. Slight pause. All is momentarily calm. Then Hilary is suddenly up and pacing about in an agitated state

Hilary Hang on a minute — hang on a minute — we're still two down. Where are Vicky and her sister? Haven't they come with you two?
Maggie No, they decided to get a taxi straight from Vicky's to the station.
Hilary (*fraught*) Great!! Bloody great!! What are we going to do if they don't get here soon? (*Looking at her watch*) We've got less than five minutes. Mind you, Vicky's quite punctual normally. I just hope they haven't got stuck in traffic or anything. We should give her a ring on her mobile.

Vicky strolls on arm in arm with Andrew. Andrew wears smart casual gear and sunglasses, and he also has a small overnight bag with him. Vicky looks the height of fashion with a short skirt and killer high heels

Hilary has her back to Vicky and Andrew. The others are facing the duo

Hilary (*anxiously*) Siobhan, you know Vicky's number, don't you? Just give her a buzz on your mobile, will you, to check she's going to arrive on time.
Siobhan (*holding her mobile to her ear — saying over Hilary's shoulder to Vicky*) Vicky, are you going to arrive on time?
Vicky (*responding solemnly*) Most definitely, Siobhan.

Hilary spins round, sees Vicky and Andrew. She laughs sheepishly. The others view Andrew with interest

Hilary (*hugging Vicky*) Vicky. I'm so glad you've made it in time.
Vicky Hi Hilary. (*Proudly announcing to all*) This is Andrew, everyone.
Andrew Hello, ladies. It's nice to meet you at last. I've heard so much about you all.
Vicky (*looking up at him*) Yes, he was dying to meet you.
Siobhan It's nice to meet you too, Andrew. We've heard a lot about you, although it must seem a bit overpowering meeting all of Vicky's friends at once like this.

Andrew Yes, it does feel a bit like coming into the lion's den ——
Yvonne (*interrupting in a jolly-hockey-sticks tone of voice*) But the
good news is we don't bite! Well, I don't, you know. (*With a forced
laugh*) Not till I'm cornered at any rate ... (*She laughs again*)

*Andrew steps towards Yvonne — invading her body space a bit too much
for her liking — she steps back as he steps forward*

Andrew Really? Well, I've always had a thing for aggressive women.
Yvonne (*stepping back nervously*) I wouldn't say I was aggressive,
more ...
Andrew (*stepping forward again*) Dominant?
Yvonne (*stepping back again*) Dominant — no, no — er ... certainly
not ...
Vicky (*laughing*) Oh, Andrew, stop winding her up, will you. He's such
a tease.

*Hilary grabs Vicky and steers her away from Andrew. Andrew makes
chit chat with Siobhan in the background. Yvonne and Maggie nosily
observe Vicky's new man*

Hilary (*hissing*) Vicky, Vicky, where is Chloe? It's lovely to meet
Andrew, and it's really romantic that he's come to wave you off and
all that, but we are now cutting it a bit fine. (*She checks her watch*)
The train's due in a couple of minutes.
Vicky Last-minute hitch I'm afraid, the baby hasn't been too well so
Chloe can't make it ...
Hilary (*fuming*) Oh for God's sake ——
Vicky (*interrupting*) But never fear. I've managed to find a last-minute
replacement for the team. Great walker, really fit ...
Hilary (*relieved*) Oh that is brilliant, Vicky. (*Gabbling on*) Who is it?
That explains why she's a bit late ... Oh — I know, it's that girl who
works in the office at your school, isn't it? She really wanted to be in
the team, didn't she? (*Checking her watch*) Mind you, she'll have to
get a flaming move on you know ——
Vicky (*interrupting*) No, no, no — it's not a she ...
Hilary Pardon?
Vicky It's a he. (*Slight pause. Vicky beams at Hilary*) It's Andrew. Isn't
that great?

*Vicky and Hilary turn slowly to look at Andrew. Hilary is totally
gobsmacked; Vicky is ecstatic. Vicky rushes over to Andrew*

Andrew I don't know about you, darling, but I'm going to have to make a dash to the little boys' room ...

Vicky (*giggling*) And I'll have to go to the little girls' room. (*To the others*) Could you just mind the bags? We'll be back in a minute.

Andrew and Vicky dash off hand in hand and giggling like a couple of teenagers

All the others rush up to Hilary expectantly

Siobhan Well, well?

Hilary (*grumpily*) Well what?

Maggie What were you and Vicky discussing?

Siobhan Yes, come on Hilary. If looks could kill!

Hilary What's that supposed to mean?

Yvonne The way you were looking at Andrew just now. (*She laughs*) For God's sake, he's only come to wave her off that's all. Anyone would think he was coming with us! (*She laughs heartily*)

Hilary (*matter-of-factly*) He is!

Yvonne stops laughing

Yvonne What?

Hilary He is coming with us.

Yvonne (*outraged*) But he's a man!

Hilary Top marks for observational skills there, Yvonne. That university education of yours wasn't a complete waste of time then.

Yvonne But he's a man.

Much ad-libbed consternation from the group: "what's going on", "bloody cheek" etc.

Hilary (*loudly silencing the others*) He is not just coming with us — he is walking with us as well.

Yvonne (*shouting angrily*) BUT HE'S A MAN!

Siobhan Yes, yes, Yvonne, we've all got the message, thank you, there's no need to shout.

Yvonne But this is a women-only weekend, girls only, remember? God, I am really pissed off now! (*She stomps to the other end of the platform*)

Maggie Is that allowed, Hilary? Isn't this a women-only event?

Hilary No. It is a fundraising event for a breast cancer charity. All and sundry are encouraged to participate, even men. (*Shouting across to Yvonne*) So we can't bar him from coming on those grounds.

Yvonne (*shouting back*) Well, find some other bloody grounds, and quick! For crying out loud — I've managed to get rid of my flaming men for the weekend and now I've got to put up with someone else's!

Siobhan Now come on, girls, let's look on the positive side. We've got a full team again, and it means we haven't wasted any money on unused tickets and hotel accommodation.

Maggie (*horrified*) Hotel accommodation!! But we're all sharing rooms! Who wants to get stuck in a family room with them?

Yvonne They're probably at it in the loos right now ...

Siobhan Now stop that!

Maggie It's a bit off, though, isn't it, Hilary, springing it on us like this at the last minute?

Hilary I can't criticize Vicky for that. Her sister's baby isn't well and Andrew is the last-minute replacement.

Yvonne But we're the Cheshire Cats, remember? All catwomen together!

Hilary Well, we'll just have to be the Cheshire Cats and the Tomcat now, won't we?

Maggie But what will he wear?

Yvonne Who bloody cares? What I want to know is, can we get him neutered on the train down?

Yvonne, Maggie, and Siobhan sit down as one on a station bench, arms folded glumly. Hilary addresses them

Hilary Look, I know he's a man. (*Looking pointedly at Yvonne*) But he is fit, he can walk, he can raise money — and Vicky's happy. Let's look at it like that shall we?

Maggie
Siobhan } (*together; half-heartedly*) Yeah ...

Slight pause

Yvonne (*loudly*) But he's a *man*! A bloody man!

Hilary
Siobhan } (*together*) We know! We know!
Maggie

Yvonne (*standing; confronting Hilary*)
> A man in our team — it's ruining my day.
> I am not putting up with this — no way!
> When we had that big team talk,
> And we all agreed to walk the Walk
> You didn't mention men at all.

"Girls only" you said, so call
Me stupid or a daft old bat —
There's no way he's a Cheshire Cat!
A bloody man's coming with us on our weekend away!
Why does he want to come?
Hang on — maybe's he's gay!

Hilary Oh come off it, Yvonne, what a daft thing to say!

Yvonne   But he's a man, not a girl,
And it's ruining my day!
A Tomcat will not do for me —
It's women only, don't you see?
We're pink and girly little stars
All off to London in our bras.
He can stay at home he can, 'cos after all —
He is a MAN!
A bloody man!
A man in our team — walking with us as well!
I am not having this — it's my idea of hell!
You can call me stupid or a daft old bat
But there is no way he's a Cheshire Cat!
(*After a pause*; *shouting*) He's a man! A bloody man!

Hilary
Siobhan } (*together; shouting*) We know, we know!
Maggie

Vicky and Andrew enter unseen as the girls are shouting

Vicky What do we all know?

The group fall silent and look at Yvonne pointedly

Yvonne (*sheepishly*) We all know that Andrew is coming on the walk
with us.
Siobhan (*diplomatically*) It's really kind of you to step in at the last
minute, Andrew.
Andrew "Step" being the operative word, ladies. We'll all be putting
our best foot forward this weekend, won't we? Or should that be
"breast foot forward"?

Vicky giggles at the joke. The others just glare at him

Vicky We certainly shall, darling.

Andrew (*staring deep into Vicky's eyes*) And if everyone's legs are as luscious as yours are, Vicky, London has a real treat in store tonight.

Vicky gazes back into his eyes and there is a lust-charged moment of silence between them, and an awkward moment amongst the others who are watching this

Maggie (*breaking the silence with a nervous laugh*) Ha ha ha. I don't think my legs could ever compete with Vicky's! I could be a good prop forward with mine ... ha ha ha ...

Yvonne (*supportively patting Maggie's leg*) So long as they can walk all those miles, Maggie, that is all that matters.

Hilary (*briskly*) Right folks, come on. Have we all got our bags? Get all your stuff together — this train is due any minute now.

The girls gather their belongings. Right on cue a platform announcement is made. They all listen intently except Vicky and Andrew who kiss and cuddle

A series of very garbled train messages fades in and out again

Announcer The train now approaching platform ... is the ... for London Euston calling at ... and ...

All look baffled again by the announcement. Slight pause, then another announcement is made, this time crystal clear

This is a colleague announcement. John — I'm still waiting for that ten quid you owe me. I repeat, still waiting for that ten quid.

There is the sound of a train approaching the platform. The Lights slowly start to fade down

The girls stand in a line on the edge of the imaginary platform, luggage in hand, and look R expectantly up the line together. Hilary is at the end of the line nearest to Vicky and Andrew, the snogging duo, who are L. She glances over, nudging Siobhan who in a chain reaction of a move nudges Maggie who nudges Yvonne. The girls are all now looking the other way down the platform at the snogging couple

Yvonne (*disgusted*) Pass the sick bucket perlease!

After a pointed pause the girls turn to look R up the line again for the train. The sound of the train approaching the platform reaches a climax as the Lights fade out ...

In the black-out we hear the sound of a train stopping, then leaving the platform, and then chugging along

SCENE 2

The train to London

The Lights come up on the rearranged seats which are now placed in groups of four and staggered either side of the imaginary train aisle. On one side of the aisle two seats face two seats with a table in between them. In the other group the seats are placed two behind two facing the audience

Maggie and Siobhan sit on the front two seats facing the audience. Maggie is in the aisle seat; Siobhan occupies the window seat next to Maggie. In the group of four seats with the table, Yvonne and Hilary sit next to each other in the seats that face the audience. Yvonne is in the aisle seat; Hilary is in the window seat. The other two seats on the other side of the table are unoccupied but have some of Vicky and Andrew's belongings on them. The girls' bags are under their chairs and magazines, newspapers, bottles of water, sweets etc. are on the tables. Vicky and Andrew are offstage

Slight pause. The sound effect of the train trundling along continues

Yvonne (*moodily staring ahead; then loudly and sullenly*) Right then, own up. Whose bloody bright idea was it to have a lucky draw for the train seats?

Maggie (*shouting over the train noise to Yvonne*) Mine! There wasn't a lot of time, and it seemed the fairest thing to do in the circumstances ...

The train noise fades out now as the scene continues. It can be faded up and down as appropriate

Yvonne I notice that you've conveniently ended up over there, Maggie, while I'm sat over here directly opposite the star-crossed lovers!

Hilary (*looking up from her magazine*) Stop whining, will you? I'm over here as well!

Yvonne Yes, but I'm directly opposite HIM! If he leers at me or raises his eyebrow at me one more time I'll bloody well chuck him off at the next stop ...

Hilary Calm down, will you ...?

Siobhan They've gone to the refreshment carriage. What was it he said as they were going?

Yvonne (*mimicking Andrew*) "We may be some time, ladies!" And why does he raise his eyebrow at me all the time? Is that supposed to be attractive? I just don't know what Vicky sees in him.

Maggie (*wistfully*) He's full of charm though, isn't he?

Yvonne Is that what you call it? More like smarm ...

Maggie We're just not used to it any more, Yvonne. Wasn't your husband like that when you first met him?

Yvonne Never! He had a certain sort of rugged allure, but I would never have called it charm! I find all that smoothness a bit creepy. Give me a bit of rough any day.

Hilary Well we know who to pass all the football louts over to when we're in London then, Yvonne.

Yvonne No, not louts. Just people with a bit of edge. I like a man who's got more than his fair share of testosterone.

Siobhan I'd say Andrew's got his fair share of testosterone. He can't keep his hands off Vicky.

Yvonne And she is all over him like a rash.

Maggie It's quite sweet really. They're besotted with each other, and they don't care who knows it.

Yvonne I personally don't want to know any more, thank you. I would prefer to remain in blissful ignorance of their feelings, not to mention gropings.

Hilary Lighten up a bit will you, Yvonne. Look, when they come back we'll play a game or something, you know, try to keep them occupied a bit.

Yvonne What do you suggest? Strip Poker?

Siobhan How about Kiss and Tell?

Hilary Or Spin the Bottle?

Maggie (*seriously*) What about a game of Jenga?

Yvonne
Hilary } (*together; loudly and incredulously*) JENGA?!
Siobhan

Yvonne } (*together*) On a train?
Hilary

Maggie (*taking out an astonishing variety of travel games from her bag*) Why not? I've brought some games with me. They definitely keep people occupied, especially Jenga, even if it is just picking up all the pieces when it falls down.

The train brakes squeal slightly. Maggie lurches over to pass the game to Hilary and Yvonne

You want to keep that busy boy's hands occupied, don't you?

Yvonne (*snatching it out of Maggie's hands*) Brilliant thinking there, Maggie.

Maggie You and Hilary set it up and look like you're having a game. When they get back you can suggest they have a go as well.

Maggie lurches back to her seat

Yvonne This will keep their hot little hands busy.

Hilary Right, come on then — get the pieces out — let's get cracking ...

Hilary and Yvonne are now occupied with setting up the Jenga tower. Under the next, they play it together

Maggie (*to Siobhan*) Do you know what I'd like to do on the Sunday after the walk? Go to the Tate Modern art gallery. I was hoping to go with Vicky but it looks as though she'll be fully occupied now. Do you fancy coming?

Siobhan I'd rather hit the shops if that's OK, Maggie — art galleries aren't really my scene.

Maggie is a bit disappointed. Siobhan sees, so adds diplomatically

Tell you what — if you spend a couple of hours with me at the shops then I'll come with you to the Tate — is it a deal?

Maggie Thanks, Siobhan. It's always nicer to go with someone else I think, sharing the experience and all that.

Siobhan How's your Access course going anyway?

Maggie Well, I'm hoping to start my art degree soon if my marks are good enough ... and if everything's OK ... (*Her voice trails off*)

Siobhan Everything's OK? What do you mean?

Maggie Oh nothing really, I've just got to finish my project work and sort out all my finances, that's all. There's more to being a student than studying!

Siobhan You'll have a ball. How exciting, being a mature student!

Maggie I don't know about mature, more like decrepit! I feel so old. When I went for my interview the other girls all looked so young!

Siobhan But you're not old. You're still a young woman. And just think of all your life experience compared to theirs, think what you've got to offer.

Maggie But Siobhan, don't you ever wish you were eighteen again?

Siobhan No way. I was spotty, no confidence, grateful if a geeky boy looked at me. Believe me, you'll be fine, Maggie.

Maggie Anyway, talking of art, I want you to all contribute a little something to my current project.

Siobhan Oh my God, we won't have to draw anything will we? Oh the shame, I'm useless at art.

Maggie No, no — it's nothing like that. It's more how you all feel about ...

Hilary and Yvonne's Jenga tower collapses. There is sudden uproar at the table. Hilary is triumphant as she has beaten Yvonne

Hilary (*standing, arms triumphantly raised in the air*) Yes! Yes! I haven't lost my touch!

Yvonne For God's sake, Hilary. Calm down and sit down. You are soooo competitive!

Hilary (*sitting down*) So are you! You can't deny you thought you had it in the bag then.

Yvonne It is *just* a game of Jenga.

Hilary (*reconstructing the Jenga tower*) Oh no — it's not *just* a game of Jenga — this is Jenga on a *train* — for which a much higher level of skill is needed. You know I'm right ... ha ha ...

Yvonne (*rattily*) Yes, I know it is Jenga on a *train* — for which a much higher level of skill may or may not be needed — that is a debatable point ...

Hilary All right, all right, keep your hair on ... no need to have a tantrum ...

Yvonne But I also know that the whole point of setting this up was not to actually play, but to just look as though we were bloody playing. So in that respect you are very much the loser, did you hear that? (*Spelling it out, hitting Hilary on the head with a piece of Jenga as she spits out each letter*) L .O. S. E. R. Loser! And therefore, I am the winner! (*She is momentarily triumphant*)

Andrew and Vicky enter down the train aisle from the back of the stage

Yvonne sits back in her chair quickly as she hears them coming

The noise of the train fades up as Andrew and Vicky enter. They totter down the aisle. Yvonne and Hilary furtively start stacking the Jenga bricks again into a tower. Train noise fades down

Andrew (*standing behind Hilary and Yvonne, his arm round Vicky*) Hello ladies, and what have we here then? A little something to keep us all amused on the journey down?
Vicky Oh! It's Jenga isn't it?
Andrew Jenga! On a train?
Yvonne (*sullenly*) Yes, Andrew. On a train.
Hilary *Far* more difficult to play on a train.

Hilary and Yvonne exchange looks — and Hilary carries on building the tower

Yvonne and I have just had a game.
Andrew Who won?

Pause. Yvonne and Hilary stare at each other again

Yvonne (*in a petulant tone of voice; looking away*) Hilary did actually.

Hilary makes a triumphant gesture

Andrew I'm surprised you didn't win, Yvonne. After all, you've got such a *dominant* personality!

Yvonne glares at him

Hilary So Andrew, how do you fancy *dominating* Vicky in the next round and playing her then?
Vicky (*giggling*) Oh, Hilary. Stop that.
Andrew (*still standing with Vicky; looking deep into her eyes*) How do you fancy playing some games in public, then, sweetie? We've already played quite a few in private after all.
Vicky And I've enjoyed every one of them, darling.

Another lust-charged moment and momentary silence between the duo. Yvonne looks appalled. Andrew breaks the moment by briskly rubbing his hands together and becoming almost business-like in his approach to the game. He remains standing. Vicky sits down opposite Hilary

Andrew OK then, let's get started, shall we? If I remember rightly you have to have pretty nimble fingers for this.

Yvonne Well I'm sure you have all the necessary attributes to be a star player then, Andrew.

The group giggle audibly at this remark. Andrew looks round at them with a raised eyebrow. They all stop as one

Andrew I'm sure I have, Yvonne, and I fully intend to play you in the next round. I bet your fingers are really strong and firm, just like you. (*Bending to whisper loudly in Yvonne's ear*) I bet they've spanked a few bottoms in their time!
Yvonne Bloody cheek, who do you think you're talking to ——

There is a loud squeal of brakes. Yvonne is interrupted and she and Hilary lurch forward across the table, knocking the restacked tower of Jenga flying over the table and on to the floor. The train then chugs along

Vicky (*dramatically*) Oh no.
Andrew Oh yes, oh dear. (*To Vicky*) I suppose somebody will have to get on the floor now and grovel round your feet and pick all those pieces up. But if I remember rightly, Vicky, you have rather ticklish feet so it should be quite stimulating. I can't wait ...

Andrew gets down on the floor, his bum up in the air in the aisle, and starts foraging round people's feet. Yvonne looks horrified

Vicky (*giggling*) He's right, you know. I've got terribly ticklish feet, and thighs!
Hilary (*holding up her hand to silence Vicky*) Too much information, Vicky. I don't really want to know what Andrew has done with your thighs.

Yvonne squeals loudly and lifts her knees up. Andrew has found her ticklish spot

Vicky (*giggling*) He is such a tease, isn't he? So playful ...
Yvonne (*gritted teeth*) Yes, he is, isn't he? So playful. A bit like a dog really, a great big randy dog ...

Andrew's bottom is stuck up in the air as he searches under the table for bits of Jenga. Yvonne slaps it firmly. His head bounces up and hits the underside of the table

Siobhan Listen, folks. Maggie was just telling me about her art course, weren't you, Maggie?

Maggie I was just explaining to Siobhan how I hoped you would all be part of my current art project.

Vicky We'd love to. What's the project about?

Maggie Actually, it's about this walk, and I've called it "Moonwalking".

Ad-libbed expressions of "that sound interesting" etc. from all except Andrew who is still picking up pieces of Jenga

It's part of my art exhibition at the end of the Access course I'm on, and one thing I'd really like to include is ——

Yvonne screams loudly, interrupting Maggie. Andrew's hand comes up between Yvonne's legs with a piece of Jenga which he places on the table

Yvonne (*regaining her composure*) Sorry, Maggie, carry on ...

Maggie I'd really love to include people's reasons for taking part in the walk. I know it's a bit of fun, all girls together on a weekend away ——

Yvonne (*interrupting and pointing at Andrew's bottom*) Plus one boy.

Andrew comes out from under the table. The last remaining pieces of Jenga are in his hand. He is on his knees next to Yvonne

Andrew I'll have you know that I'm all man, Yvonne!

Vicky Oh stop teasing her, Andrew, and sit down.

Andrew sits down next to Vicky. Yvonne glares at him

Maggie (*standing*) I know people have really personal reasons for taking part in this event, so I want you all to take one of these blank postcards each ... (*she busies herself getting postcards and a wad of coloured pens out of her bag*) ... and I'd like you to write a quick couple of sentences about why you're participating in the walk. I'm just after a gut feeling really — don't think too much about it, just write what's in your heart.

The group chatters initially. They all take a pen and a postcard from Maggie. There is a momentary silence. A pensive mood takes over

The train chugs away in the background. Maggie sits down again. All have their pens poised and are just about to write when ...

Siobhan (*loudly interrupting people's thoughts*) Do you want this in capitals, Maggie? My handwriting is terrible!

Hilary and Yvonne groan loudly

Andrew She has got a point, you know. So is mine.

Another groan

Siobhan (*to the group*) Now, come on, it's got to be legible, hasn't it?
Hilary Well, I've got lovely handwriting ... for goodness' sake.
Vicky And I've started now ...
Maggie (*raising her voice over the others*) OK then — OK! Capitals, please, folks, if you feel your handwriting isn't up to scratch.
Yvonne Is that the last technical hitch then? Can we now put pen to paper? Or does anyone have any last wishes regarding grammar, punctuation and vocabulary?
All Oooooooh!!!!

Maggie stands and shushes them. She takes control and announces to all loudly over the hubbub

Maggie Let the writing begin! (*She sits*)

All heads go down and they write. There is complete silence except for the faint chugging of the train. There should be a marked change of atmosphere. All inhabit their own private worlds as they consider, write and then read their thoughts to themselves. Those in the window seats stare out, lost in thought. Andrew and Vicky silently exchange cards and read them

The sound of the train comes up to fill the stage with noise. It reaches a climax and there is a sudden Black-out

CURTAIN

ACT III — WALKING

NB: The alternative dialogue and stage directions provided in some scenes are for the ensemble version of Act III, which allows for a larger cast

Scene 1

London at night

Traffic noise can be heard as Hilary appears alone in the spotlight in her Cheshire Cats walking outfit to address her unseen Cheshire Cats team. Car doors should slam at appropriate points in the monologue

Hilary (*much in the manner of a teacher talking to children in a nursery*) Now, can you just check that you've left your valuables in the hotel, and that you have got some money in your bumbags for the taxis back to the hotel at the end of the walk. Have you all got your race number with you, girls — yes — and you, Andrew? Well if you haven't then you won't be allowed to enter, will you? The race organizers are very strict about that. Oh you've found it. Well what number are you then, Andrew? What was that ... sixty-nine? Very funny ... No, no ... you can all stop giggling now. I know you weren't giggling, Yvonne ... and yes, yes, you're right, it wasn't that funny. Remember to put plenty of Vaseline on those pressure points, girls. No, Andrew, I don't really want to know where you've put yours ... Oh, here come the taxis.

Sound of taxis pulling up and car doors opening

And remember, we'll all meet up at the race marquee near the food line. Vicky, you and Andrew get in with Yvonne and Maggie. In you go. No, NO Yvonne, I can't swap you with someone else, just get in and stop moaning, will you.

Sound of car door slamming

(*Waving them off; with false jollity*) See you there then! (*Relieved*) Thank goodness — that's got rid of Handy Andy for the next half hour. Just me and you now, Siobhan. A nice bit of peace and quiet

before the walk. (*She flags a cab down excitedly*) Come on, come on
— TAXI, TAXI! ... Oh, look, look ... Here's ours.

Sound effect of car pulling up

Come on, let's go ... London's streets, here we come!

Black-out

*The sound of doors slamming and the taxi pulling away. There is the
sound of a car motoring for a few seconds and fading into the distance.
Silence for a couple of seconds, then suddenly a very loud sound effect
of the marquee festivities to open Scene 2*

SCENE 2

The Pink Walk Marquee

*An Aerobics Instructor immediately blows his/her whistle sharply.
Bright coloured lights and loud dance music snap up. He/she is here to
put the waiting walkers — who at this stage are the audience — through
their warm-up paces in the Walk Marquee. He/she gets the audience to
participate as much as possible with arm and leg stretching exercises,
as many as possible on their feet*

Aerobics Instructor (*booming out instructions*) Right, girls ... And
boys ... come on now, come on. Concentrate, con-cen-trate on those
moves ... don't forget we have got to warm up those beautifully toned
leg muscles if we don't want to injure ourselves en route — on your
feet, yes on your feet if you can — that's the way — just copy me
now — great. There is a long way to go tonight, remember — so if
you've already eaten that lovely pasta that's been provided to fuel
you round the walk then join in as we streeeetch, two, three. (*He/
she bounces over to another side of the stage and turns and stretches
again*) One, two, three ... really streeeetch those muscles now ... Now
come on over there — get those arms in the air — really stretch up
now. (*Getting as much of a routine in with the audience as he/she can
at this point. Once the routine is well underway he/she points offstage
to an unseen group*) Oh come on you lot over there — I want to see a
lot more enthusiasm from you ...

*He/she cartwheels off in a flashy show of gymnastic ability through
one exit*

Hilary and Siobhan enter from the opposite direction carrying food in foil trays, and wearing bum bags carrying their essentials. Siobhan has a small camera and is excitedly taking photos as and when she can. Hilary carries a huge bottle of water. They are wearing their race outfits, cat's ears that light up, and cat's tails. They are an unintentionally comic version of Vicky's sexy outfit as seen in Act I. They also have their official race numbers on yellow card pinned to their thighs which they check self-consciously every now and then to check they are still on OK

They excitedly pick their way across a very crowded marquee and try to find a bit of space for the group to sit down so they need to create this atmosphere with their actions — ideally using the audience as parts of the crowd when they can

Hilary (*looking around with awe*) Bloody hell! I didn't think that it would be so crowded in here did you, Siobhan?

Siobhan Not really. (*Politely to a person seated in the Marquee — ideally an audience member*) Sooo sorry, did I tread on your foot then? Are you all right ... yes ... it *is* incredibly full, isn't it? Have you travelled far to come tonight? ... Where are you from? (*She waits for a reply and repeats it*) Really??? Did you have a good journey?? Oh that's good ... no missed connections then?

Hilary drags Siobhan away

Hilary (*hissing to Siobhan*) All right, all right. That's the tenth bloody person you have had that conversation with in this marquee. Come on — let's move on, please ... It's all right for that lot ... (*Indicating the audience*) They've all got good seats, we're still looking for somewhere to park our bums!

Siobhan I can't help being polite, can I? (*Jovially to the audience member*) Well, good luck then ... Yes ... yes ... that's right ... (*laughing*) ... might see you on the walk on the way round ... bye ...

They continue to daintily pick their way to a space on the marquee floor — suddenly pointing to a space in the middle of the stage. They are slightly hysterical with the excitement of it all

(*Excitedly*) Here we are, here we are, a little gap in a sea of faces ... Let's park ourselves here if we can squeeze in ... (*To an unseen seated walker*) Excuse me, thanks ... (*She settles herself down*)

Hilary remains standing

Hilary Thank goodness for that, this must be the first part of the challenge — finding a space to sit down in.

Siobhan (*looking round, taking photographs — very excited*) Whoopee!! I'm feeling quite festive now, it is just amazing how many people are here. It's great ... just like one big party. (*Looking up at Hilary*) Sit down, Hilary, and save your legs ...

Hilary I'd better stay standing in case the others don't see us when they get here. (*Checking her watch*) Their taxi left before ours — I would have thought they would be here by now ... (*She takes a mouthful of the food and looks disgusted*) God — that pasta is a bit dry, isn't it? Where's me water ... (*She starts to glug the water down enthusiastically*)

Siobhan Now don't be drinking too much water, Hilary, or you'll be stopping at all the loos in the first ten minutes of the race ...

Hilary (*stopping; nearly choking*) Oh God, yes — I'll lose time if I end up doing that, and I really want to do a good time if I can. I've got to do a personal best ——

Maggie and Yvonne enter and interrupt Hilary by shouting. They are also carrying food trays. Maggie has a bag with her in which to collect all their rubbish up when they leave the stage at the end of this scene. Ideally they should enter through the audience if possible — shouting excitedly

Maggie (*shouting*) Hilary, Hilary ...

Yvonne (*waving and weaving her way through the crowd*) Yoo hoo, girls, girls ... make room for us ...

Siobhan gets to her feet and waves

Siobhan Come on, Yvonne, Maggie — come on girls, over here ... we've saved you a little space — thought we'd lost you before we started!

On her way Yvonne accidentally treads on someone's foot (again — an audience member if possible). She looks down disdainfully in response to their unheard remark

Yvonne Excuse me, excuse me. So sorry — and *yes*, I *did* look where I was putting my big feet thank you very much. (*Going to tip-toe on,* *and then looking back shocked*) Well! There's no need for that sort of language — really ... (*To Maggie*) Did you hear what she said to me then ... the cheeky bloody so-and-so ...

Maggie (*embarrassed*) Come on, Yvonne, get a move on will you, nearly there now ... (*Apologizing to an audience member*) So sorry — it's been a long day for everyone, hasn't it? ... (*She starts to forage in her bum bag*) Do you need a plaster for that at all? I've got one here (*She produces a selection of plasters*) ... Oh — you're all right, are you? That's great. Might see you on the way round then. (*She pushes Yvonne towards Hilary and Siobhan*)

Yvonne and Maggie search for a place to sit. Hilary still stands. There are many excited girly noises and much ad-libbing. They all jiggle about making space for each other

If I could just squeeze in here that will be great. (*She sits*)

Yvonne (*bossily*) Come on, budge up will you, budge up, I can barely get a buttock into that space ... (*She squeezes in*)

Hilary still stands and looks round the marquee as she munches her pasta. The Aerobics Instructor's voice booms out and they all look out over the audience's heads towards the unseen stage he/she is on. The voice shouts out exercise instructions which they excitedly follow in unison

Voice of Aerobics Instructor Come on now, folks, on your feet — *all of you* ... Let's have some real strutting going on now while you warm up, and all feel free to sing along if you want to ...

Music blares out: "These Boots Were Made for Walking". They all jump up. The voice of the Aerobics Instructor gives instructions for various stretching and warm-up exercises. The girls all follow

The Aerobics Instructor shouts out an instruction to all touch their toes. All except Maggie do so. Unnoticed by the others Maggie does a silent prayer before she attempts to touch her toes. Maggie's old back problem kicks in again and she cannot straighten up. She is at eye level with Yvonne. Yvonne then straightens up. Hilary and Siobhan are oblivious to Maggie's difficulties and carry on with the warm-up enthusiastically

Maggie (*hissing — her head down by her knees*) Yvonne, Yvonne ...

Yvonne (*looking down at Maggie*) What ... what's the problem? ... Oh no ... it's your back, isn't it?

Maggie Don't say anything to the others. Just help me straighten up ...
I'll be OK once I'm upright ...

*Yvonne starts to gingerly help Maggie straighten up. The straightening
up procedure should be nice and gentle until ...*

Hilary (*suddenly staring out at the audience*) OH NO — I don't believe
it!! Look at that!

*Yvonne and Maggie think Hilary has twigged Maggie's back problem
and should look suitably horrified*

Vicky (*off, calling loudly*) Hilary! Yoo hoo! Hilary ...

All the group now look expectantly in the direction of Vicky's voice

All (*in unison in a loud and horrified tone*) Oh ... My ... God ...

*Vicky and Andrew enter, again ideally as far back as possible and
through the audience. Andrew is beautifully made up and dressed in
team bra, beautiful blonde curly wig tied in bunches, long black tights
and a flouncy pink tutu with a pink Barbie backpack. He bounces to the
group and struts up and down like a model on a catwalk, eyeing up the
audience as he reaches the sides of the stage and turning on his heel to
continue strutting his stuff. He is camping it up big time*

Original version:	*Ensemble version:*
Andrew ends up standing in front of Yvonne. She slowly looks him up and down	*Andrew ends up standing in front of the Aerobics Instructor. He/ she slowly looks him up and down*
Yvonne Not very Nike are we ...? **Andrew** (*tossing his bunches; in a camp voice*) George at Asda actually.	**Aerobics Instructor** Not very Nike are we ...? **Andrew** (*tossing his bunches; in a camp voice*) George at Asda actually.
	Aerobics Instructor shrugs, laughs, and then notices a part of the crowd not exercising enough. He/ she shouts into the wings

> **Aerobics Instructor** Come on, you lot — put a bit of backbone into it! Call that stretching? I'll show you how to stretch!
>
> *He/she cartwheels off*

All the girls except Yvonne have a laugh at Andrew's outfit. All are now shouting loudly to be heard over the background music

Hilary (*laughing*) What does he look like?

Siobhan Very nice if you ask me — at least we're an all girl group now!

Hilary (*to Vicky*) What took you so long to get here?

Vicky We were just outside the marquee putting the finishing touches to Andrew's outfit for the night. We wanted to surprise you all ... (*Giggling*) What do you think?

Andrew strikes a feminine pose and looks at Hilary archly. Yvonne tuts and looks disgusted

Hilary Very nice, Andrew, especially the hair — it really suits you.

Andrew (*toying with his locks*) Well, you know what they say, Hilary, blondes have more fun, and as this is a girly night I just wanted to feel more in touch with my feminine side ...

Maggie (*laughing*) Well — I think you look lovely, Andrew, very colourful ...

Siobhan Very striking. (*Enthusiastically and practically checking out the tutu*) What a well-made outfit that is, did you make it yourself? So feminine ...

Yvonne (*disgusted*) He looks like a flaming transvestite! Bit of a cross dresser then, are you, Andrew?

Andrew (*very camp now to annoy Yvonne*) Not really — this is my first time, but I could grow to like it! What do you think, Vicky, is it a turn on for you? Would you like to ... (*thrusting his hips forward suggestively*) ... toss me bunches for me?

Vicky Give us a kiss and I'll tell you. (*She runs over to him giggling*)

Andrew grabs Vicky and bends her over his knee in a long dramatic kiss done totally for effect and to annoy Yvonne. Yvonne looks horrified. The others whoop encouragement and giggle

Yvonne (*walking over to the snogging duo and shouting over the general hilarity in horror*) No, no, stop that ... I'm sorry ... if he is

going to carry on like that all night I ... well ... I! A man in our team
... dressed as a woman ... Kissing my friend ... a man in our team ...
God — he is ruining my night!

Hilary Oh stop it, Yvonne, you're just jealous 'cos he's got a better
cleavage than you have ...

The lovers' embrace ends

Andrew (*in a deep masculine tone of voice to Vicky*) Well thanks very
much, luv, that were grand!

Vicky (*gasping for breath*) Mmmmmm, that was a new experience. I've
never been snogged by someone wearing more make-up than me —
but it was very enjoyable ... you ... you little minx, you!!

The sound of the music in the background rises in volume

Original version:	*Ensemble version:*
The Aerobics Instructor's voice booms out again	*The Aerobics Instructor bounces on stage again*
Aerobics Instructor's Voice Now then, folks — it's time for all the people in the yellow group to make their way to the start line ...	**Aerobics Instructor** Now then, folks — it's time for all the people in the yellow group to make their way to the start line, so come on — get your stuff together ...

Maggie (*shouting*) The yellow group — that's us isn't it, Hilary? It is,
isn't it?

Hilary Yes, that's us, the yellow group, that's us. Come on, girls, put all
your rubbish in the bag and gather all your stuff together — we'll chuck
it in the bin on the way out ...

*The girls quickly put their rubbish in Maggie's bag and busy themselves
checking their belongings, race numbers etc.*

Aerobics Instructor's Voice Remember, folks, different colour groups depending on your predicted walking times, just the yellow group for the half marathon to the starting line please. Now remember to	**Aerobics Instructor** Remember, folks, different colour groups depending on your predicted walking times, just the yellow group for the half marathon to the starting line please. Now remember to walk folks ...

walk folks ... (*Giggling slightly*) ... Or even mince if you feel like it — you know who you are — but don't run, we don't want any accidents before you start, do we?

(*Looking at Andrew*) ... Or even mince if you feel like it — but don't run, we don't want any accidents before you start now, do we?

Aerobics Instructor exits

They all babble excitedly as they realize that they are due to make their way to the start line. They start to make their way off, Maggie carrying the bag of rubbish. Hilary shouts instructions

Hilary Right folks, keep close together. Let's get as near to the front of the group so we can get off to a great start ... Come on, Cheshire Cats!

Hilary leads them out, chanting the marching song they have used in practice walks: "I don't know but I've been told ..."

The Lights snap off. The sound effect of the crowd increases in volume

Scene 3

The start line

Night sky effect. The Lights come up and the general hubbub of a crowd in the background is heard. A "Start" banner indicates the start line for the walk. In the ensemble version of the act, this is held by Marshall 1 and Marshall 2

The girls enter with Hilary leading the group on. They are shouting over the background noise of the crowd, and are all very excited

Maggie (*shivering*) Gosh, it's cold. Let's hope we get warmed up on the way round.

Original version:

Siobhan It's a great night for the walk, though. (*Looking up*) Look how clear that sky is!
Hilary Yes, it's beautiful. Not quite a full moon, but beautiful all the same.

Ensemble version:

Hilary Right. Good idea, Maggie. (*Hilary then speaks from "Now stick together..." on p.51*)

Vicky It's such a great name for the
walk isn't it? The "Moonwalk"
— such a great idea ...
Andrew And you girls walking
tonight are little stars — all of
you — little stars ...
Vicky (*looking up at him*) Oh,
darling ... how sweet of you to
say that ...
Yvonne Oh gawd ... they're at it
again ...

Hilary Right. Now stick together now folks, I'm going to lead us all as
far to the front as I can. (*Pointing to the start line, and then producing
a large flashing fairy wand which she holds aloft*) Remember, follow
the wand — have we all got that? It's a bit of extra luck for us all and
it just means we won't lose each other in the crowd.
Yvonne Where did you get that from?
Hilary Oh — I've got me contacts, you know.
Yvonne (*enviously*) Well — we might all have liked one of those.
Hilary Yvonne, who is the elected team leader of the Cheshire Cats?
Yvonne Er, you are ...
Hilary And you are?
Yvonne A team member ...
Hilary So I am the leader and you are ...?
Yvonne A follower ...
Hilary SO who needs to be seen in the crowd?
Yvonne You do ...
Hilary Precisely.

*Yvonne is downcast and sulking. Hilary looks at her and then gives her
the wand*

Oh bloody well have it then — but hold it up high, remember, so we
can all see it.

*Yvonne is thrilled. She holds the wand high, standing on tippy toe with
the others excitedly bunched round her*

(*Pushing onwards*) Come on, folks, keep pushing forward now, all
together ... Hold on to each other's tails ...
Maggie (*anxiously*) How near to the front do you want to get, Hilary?
It's just that I tend to get a bit nervous in crowds, you know, when
we're all pushed together like this.

Hilary (*forging forward, nearer to the start banner* R; *not looking behind her to see how Maggie is*) Nearly there, Maggie, nearly there. It's just so important for a good time to get off to a flying start, isn't it?

Siobhan (*concerned*) Hilary, Hilary ... just hold on, will you? Maggie doesn't look too good to me ...

Maggie falters a little. Siobhan and Vicky hold her up. Hilary is unaware as she has still not looked behind her to see how Maggie is

(*Anxiously*) Hilary, Hilary ... you will have to stop ... I need to get Maggie to the side ...

Vicky (*panicking*) Hold her up, Siobhan — I think she is going to faint ... Oh my God, she's going, she's going ... quick — grab her ...

Maggie goes to faint. Andrew steps forward decisively and sweeps her up and carries her forward, excusing himself to people in the crowd

Andrew Excuse me, let me through please, thanks folks, bit of an emergency. (*Etc.*)

Hilary still does not notice. The others follow Andrew. He seats Maggie on the floor L *and kneels alongside her*

Take deep breaths slowly, Maggie, that's it — in through your nose ... and out through your mouth, that's right, in slowly ... then out ... in ... then out ...

The other girls except Hilary anxiously form a tight semicircle behind Andrew and Maggie now and unconsciously breathe in and out as one as Andrew instructs Maggie to do so. Andrew slowly realizes and gestures to them not to stand too close

Back up a bit, girls, come on, back up — let her have a bit of air please.

They all take a step back

Yvonne Andrew, if you're going to give her the kiss of life take that bloody wig off before you do or it'll completely freak me out!

Maggie sighs loudly and deeply, and then holds her head up and smiles at the group gathered round her. They all audibly breathe a sigh of relief. Hilary impatiently checks her watch at the start banner

Hilary (*shouting over to the group*) What time do you make it, Siobhan? Siobhan? (*Unaware of the situation, shouting impatiently over to the others, she strides over to them*) ... Siobhan!

Siobhan (*miffed*) Maggie is not well, Hilary. Forget about the flaming time will you?

Vicky Calm down everyone, calm down.

Andrew (*still kneeling alongside Maggie*) I think Maggie has just had a little bit of a panic attack, but she's all right now, aren't you?

Maggie nods and smiles up at Andrew

Maggie Thanks, Andrew, I'll be fine once we get going. I just don't like big crowds that's all. I felt like I couldn't breathe then.

Siobhan Are you sure you're all right now, Maggie? Don't feel that you have to do this, you know. If you're not feeling well enough now is the time to say so ... we'll all understand, won't we, girls?

The others murmur their agreement except Hilary who is horrified by Siobhan's suggestion

Hilary NO! No no no no no NO ... (*She pushes Siobhan out of the way and kneels beside Maggie to frantically urge her to participate*) Of course she's all right, aren't you, Maggie? Come on, Maggie ... you can do it. And besides, if you faint on the way round we've all got our race numbers on, so if you're on your own and get found by the race marshalls ... well ... they'll be able to identify you, won't they? You know ... when they're bringing you round ... like in Casualty when they slap people's face and try to bring them round ... they always say their names, don't they ...?

The others all stare at Hilary silently. She realizes

Well, what are you all looking at ... What? What??

The others are hardly able to believe what they are hearing

Andrew (*disapprovingly*) Well, let's hope it doesn't come to that, eh Hilary?

Yvonne The way it's going you'll be the one getting a slap in the face, Hilary. What a bloody tactless thing to say.

Maggie gets to her feet. Hilary assists her

Maggie Please stop arguing. Come on, we're here to enjoy ourselves. I know, let's have a group hug before we start, but don't crowd me too much or I'll start fainting again ... Come on, everyone ... Come on ...

Maggie puts her arms round Yvonne and Hilary and the others join in — all stamping their feet quickly and shouting, "Group hug, group hug." They do the Cheshire Cats group hug semi squatting with their arms round each other's shoulders, and then leaping up to a big "Meeeeeeaaaaooow". Just as they do so the countdown for the start of the race begins. The group break apart excitedly and look to the start line expectantly

An unseen Race Organizer speaks over a loudspeaker

Race Organizer OK folks, we'll start the countdown from ten, and remember to walk and not run. Remember, this is a walking event. Good luck to you all, and thanks for taking part in this great event and raising funds for a very worthwhile cause.

The girls cheer; they are all ready to go now. All is well

Here we go then. (*Slowly*) Ten — nine — eight — seven ...

The countdown continues. The girls and the crowd join in. A klaxon sounds loudly at the end of the countdown. Hilary is at the front of the team — the leader again

Hilary (*shouting*) Come on, the Cheshire Cats — let's go ...

They all stride out lustily singing their training marching song, Hilary leading the chant and the walk

> I don't know but I've been told
> London's streets are paved with gold
> I don't know but it's been said
> Cheshire Cats are good in bed ...

The girls and Andrew all exit

In the ensemble version of the act the two marshalls holding the "Start" banner chat as follows:

Marshall 1 (*philosophically staring after the girls and folding up his banner*) It's a great night for the walk, isn't it? (*Looking up*) Look how clear that sky is!

Marshall 2 (*looking up and letting out a small whistle of delight*)
Yep, it's beautiful isn't it? Not quite a full moon, but beautiful all the
same.
Marshall 1 It's such a great name for the walk isn't it? The "Moonwalk"
— such a great idea ...
Marshall 2 (*pointing after the girls*) And those girls walking tonight are
little stars — all of them — little stars ...

*Slight pause. They both stare up at the stars and then they solemnly fold
up the banner*

Marshall 1 Fancy a cup of tea then? I'm bloody freezing!
Marshall 2 Good idea — but remember ...
Marshall 1 ⎫ (*together*) Walk — don't run!
Marshall 2 ⎭

*Both exit briskly in a mock walking race with each other, one carrying
the folded-up banner off*

Black-out

SCENE 4

One mile after the start of the race

*The group are still all together, Hilary striding on first with her
immaculate speed-walking style; Siobhan is second in line. Their team
race outfits are now in full view. Yvonne is limping as she tails after them
holding the wand forlornly aloft*

Siobhan (*chasing after Hilary*) Hilary, Hilary, hang on a minute, hang
on! Yvonne is limping quite badly.
Hilary (*pacing on the spot*) What, already! We've only done a flaming
mile!

The rest of the group stop and look at Yvonne. She stops completely

Yvonne God, I can't believe it! Only one mile and look at me!
Hilary (*striding over and then pacing on the spot*) Well I bloody well
can. You've got those new trainers on, haven't you? I told you not to
wear them didn't I?

Yvonne I must have pulled a muscle. We all went off so quickly at the start.

Hilary is still walking up and down on the spot as she speaks, then turns to look at the other group members. They are all still looking at Yvonne and murmuring sympathetically

Hilary (*barking out the order to them*) Keep flaming moving, you lot, or all your muscles will seize up too!

The group all snap into action like well-trained dogs and pace up and down

(*To Yvonne*) Well?

Yvonne Look, Hilary, I am not going to be able to keep up with you. If it means I will have to walk round on my own then so be it.

Maggie (*walking over to Yvonne*) Look, why don't Yvonne and I both walk round at a slower pace. You stride on out with the others. It's OK, really, we don't mind.

Yvonne nods in agreement with Maggie. Maggie is already shattered going at Hilary's pace and pants heavily

Yvonne (*thrilled*) Thanks, Maggie. There you go, Hilary, all resolved. You go on ahead.

Siobhan (*confronting Hilary while walking on the spot*) No, no, we'll all walk together. We came together and we're sticking together. We'll just have to slow it down a bit, that's all.

Hilary (*facing Siobhan while also walking on the spot*) As John McEnroe would say, "You cannot be serious"!

Siobhan I am. We can't leave them on their own.

Yvonne Oh yes you can, Siobhan. We'll be fine, there's thousands of people on the route. Just wait for us at the finish line and we'll all celebrate there.

Maggie Go on girls, we know how much that fast time means to you. You go on ahead, go on.

Siobhan Well, only if you're really sure you'll be ——

Hilary (*butting in*) Right. Come on the rest of you, let's go ...

Hilary marches off at a furious pace. Siobhan, Andrew and Vicky rush after her

Maggie (*sympathetically to Yvonne*) It must have hurt — pulling a muscle like that.

Yvonne Pulled a muscle my arse. I've got a bloody blister again because of these trainers, but I wasn't about to tell Hilary that! Have you got any plasters for my heel? I've left mine back at the hotel.

Maggie starts giggling and points to her bumbag

Maggie I've got loads in my bumbag, Yvonne, just what the doctor ordered, nice padded ones especially for blistered feet. Come on, let's go and find a bench for you to sit on while we put one on.

The two of them start to exit slowly. Yvonne is still limping quite badly

(*Stopping and looking round*) You know, the architecture in London is fabulous isn't it? I can't wait to walk through some upmarket areas. I'm sure we'll go past some beautiful properties on the way round. And I can't wait to walk alongside the Thames and look across at the Houses of Parliament at night. I'm just so excited to be walking round London at night — and you see so much more on foot, don't you?

Yvonne The speed I'm walking at the moment means you'll be able to count every brick.

Maggie Come on now, stop fretting, we'll soon have you right.

Yvonne Anyway, never mind my foot. How are you feeling now? That was a bit of a nasty turn you had before the walk started. Are you sure you're OK now?

Maggie I'm fine, just fine. It was just a bit of claustrophobia, that's all. (*She laughs nervously; then in a serious tone*) Actually, I have got something I wanted to ask you about, and I didn't have a chance back at the hotel. We all had to leave so fast to make it in time for the start of the walk. And I know I can confide in you, Yvonne. (*Slight pause — she looks a bit distressed*) Something's been bothering me and ...

Yvonne (*anxiously*) What is it?

There is a long, solemn pause. Maggie stares into space

Maggie (*very seriously*) Does my bum look big in these tracky bottoms?

Yvonne (*laughing*) Oh for God's sake, Maggie, shut up about your fat bum and find me a bench to sit on! You look fine, you daft thing.

Maggie does her nervous laugh. They start to leave the stage arm in arm, Yvonne still limping

Maggie (*pointing offstage*) Here's a bench, Yvonne, over here, come on ... you'll have to take your trainer off ... and then — how does that saying go now ...? "This plaster's too big ... this one's too small ..."

Yvonne }
Maggie } (*together; as they exit*) "And this one's just right!"

Maggie and Yvonne exit laughing. Their laughter fades

Black-out

SCENE 5

Five miles into the walk

The Lights come up on Hilary and Siobhan standing waiting in line for the loos. A sign says "5 mile mark" and there are crates of bottled water onstage. In the ensemble version of the act, Marshall 3 holds the sign and Marshall 4 hands out bottles of water to unseen walkers. A loud sound effect of toilets flushing is heard

Hilary is c clutching her groin, obviously desperate. She is doing the toilet turkey trot trying to stop herself from having an accident. Siobhan jogs gently on the spot, at ease with herself

Hilary (*desperate*) How much flaming longer have I got to wait — it's bloody typical isn't it? There's never enough ladies' loos no matter where you are!

Siobhan Really, it's your own fault that you're so desperate. You just wouldn't go at that other loo stop because you didn't want to lose any time.

Hilary (*clutching her groin*) I'll be all right ... but it's definitely on its way down ...

Siobhan Vicky and Andrew stopped so we could have done, couldn't we?

Hilary (*rattily*) Well, yes, I suppose so ... If you really wanted the star-crossed lovers' company all the way round ...

Siobhan (*thinking of Vicky and Andrew*) Mind you, I'm sure they're happier walking round on their own anyway!

Hilary They're hardly on their own are they? There are thousands of other walkers out there!

Siobhan Yes, but they might as well be on their own. Let's face it, they've only got eyes for each other haven't they? When you think about it, it's quite sweet really.

Hilary I suppose it is, in a strange, nauseating sort of way.

Siobhan Yes, it is a bit odd isn't it, watching a long-standing friend having an adolescent crush on someone in middle age. It can make you feel a bit like a voyeur, watching all that kissing and cuddling in public.

Hilary (*doing the turkey trot again*) Oh forget about the kissing and cuddling and concentrate on my bladder will you? Has that queue gone down yet? I'm starting to leak now ...

Siobhan (*calmly*) The queue has definitely gone down, Hilary, there's only ... (*She pauses as she mentally counts*) ... Fifteen more people before you now ... Don't worry, I'm holding a place for you.

Hilary Fifteen! I'll wet my knickers at this rate. God, my stomach is in agony! (*Panicking*) I can't hold it in much longer ... I just can't ...

Siobhan (*in a reasonable tone*) Mind you, it's fifteen people for five loos, so really it's only three people per cubicle isn't it?

Hilary Well let's hope they all just need a pee then. I couldn't cope with the wait if anyone's constipated.

Siobhan (*still looking offstage and mentally counting the queue*) Down to ten now ... So that's two people to go per cubicle ...

Hilary Stop it! Stop it — it's like flaming Chinese water torture! Just shout "NOW" when it's my turn will you.

Hilary is now c *doing the dance of a female deprived of the loo*

> *Ensemble version:*
>
> *Marshall 3 approaches Hilary in a jocular manner with bottles of water*
>
> **Marshall 3** Need any water, girls? Still a long way to go, you know ... you don't want to dehydrate, do you? (*He offers a bottle to Hilary*)
>
> *Hilary audibly growls and is about to bite*

Siobhan NOW!!!

Hilary dives offstage clutching her groin nearly knocking Siobhan over in her desperation to get to the loo

Hilary (*shouting as she leaves*) I'm next, I'm next — out of the way ... out of the way ...

Hilary exits

> *Ensemble version:*
>
> **Marshall 3** (*looking a bit shaken*)
> Only trying to help ...
> **Siobhan** Sorry about that. She's a
> bit fraught. I'll take a bottle for
> later, thanks. (*She takes a bottle
> from Marshall 3*)
>
> *Shaken, Marshall 3 rejoins his
> colleague*

Siobhan turns and confides in the audience

Siobhan (*sighing*) What a mate, what a pal!
But such a nark, a bossy gal
Yet she's someone that I wouldn't be without
Even though she has a tendency to shout about
Well — everything! (*She sighs*)
The trouble is she wants to be the boss
Of everything she sees, including me!
But I'm not cross about it, it's not my way.
I see her good points every day
And the good in her is wonderful to see
She's inspirational — not only just to me
But to all of us, our little team ...
The problem is she makes you want to scream!
But I'm proud she's led us all down here tonight
I'm proud we're wearing silly bras and that
                    we look a sight
Because she's made us all feel really grand
She's encouraged us to come and make a stand
For something that is good and great and true
Remembering the people we all knew ...
What a mate, what a pal!
But such a nark, a bossy gal
Yet she's someone that I wouldn't be without
Even though she has a tendency to shout about
Well — everything! (*She sighs*)

We hear a toilet flushing

Hilary (*off*) SIOBHAN!!

Hilary re-enters, a pained look on her face. She minces daintily forward with her knees together

(*Talking through clenched teeth*) Right, ready to go then?
Siobhan Are you all right there, Hilary? You look like you're in a bit of pain.
Hilary (*confessing*) God, Siobhan, that wee was so strong! It stung like hell — it was like passing acid, not water.

Siobhan looks at Hilary knowingly

Siobhan Well that was your own fault ——
Hilary (*interrupting*) Yes, yes — I know, it's my own bloody fault for hanging on to it for so long.

Original version:

Siobhan Next time why don't you just do it in your pants like Paula Radcliffe? If it's good enough for her it's good enough for you! Right — Cheshire Cats — let's go ...
Hilary (*interested*) Really? Did she *really* do it in her pants then?
Siobhan (*stopping*) Who?
Hilary Paula Radcliffe.
Siobhan Yes, and I bet she's regretted it ever since when you think about the amount of coverage the papers gave it! I mean to say ... in public ... it's not something people find attractive in a woman, is it? A man they would forgive, but a woman is another matter ... (*After a slight pause she giggles and nudges Hilary*) Mind you some men pay for that sort of thing you know ...

Ensemble version:

The Race Marshalls eavesdrop on their conversation

Next time I'll just do it in me pants like Paula Radcliffe. If it's good enough for her it's good enough for me! Right — Cheshire Cats — let's go ...

They stride off purposefully, Hilary mincing quickly in front, Siobhan laughing at her discomfort as she follows

Marshall 4 (*walking* c *and staring after them; to Marshall 3*) Do you think she does it in her pants then?
Marshall 3 Who, her? (*Indicating Hilary*)
Marshall 4 No, Paula Radcliffe.
Marshall 3 Well, she's no lady if she does, is she? I mean to say ... peeing in public ... it's not

Hilary looks confused

Golden showers, you know ...
nudge nudge, wink wink ... (*She
giggles at the thought*)
Hilary   (*genuinely confused*)
Golden showers? What do you
mean?
Siobhan   Well ... (*She goes to
explain, and then decides
against it. She leaves the stage,
muttering to herself*) There
are some things you just can't
explain to a prude so I won't
bother ... still so innocent at
your age, it's amazing — so
innocent ... come on.

Siobhan exits

Hilary is C, still thinking

Hilary   (*shouting after Siobhan
and walking off*) Siobhan,
Siobhan! Is it something to do
with global warming??

something I'd find attractive in
a woman, personally. (*Pause*)
Mind you, some people pay for
that sort of thing you know ...

*Slight pause. Marshall 4 looks
confused*

Golden showers ... You know ...
nudge nudge, wink wink ...
Marshall 4   (*confused*) Golden
showers? What do you mean?

*Marshall 3 goes to explain and
decides against it. He sees other
unseen walkers approaching*

Marshall 3   (*relieved; leaving the
stage to talk to them*) Ah ha —
Ladies, ladies — do you need
more fluids? Loads of water for
you over here if you do ...

Marshall 3 exits

Marshall 4   (*confused; shouting
after Marshall 3*) Is it something
to do with global warming??

Black-out

SCENE 6

7 miles into the walk

*Vicky and Andrew stroll on romantically arm in arm. There is the noise
of the crowds of walkers in the background*

Andrew   Seven miles down, five and a bit to go!
Vicky   I must admit that I'm starting to feel a bit guilty now.
Andrew   Why?
Vicky   All that training that the team did, and now I couldn't care less
how fast I'm walking. Hilary will be going bananas!

Andrew Let her. So long as we make it to the end in one piece we'll still collect the sponsorship money. Anyway, I thought you found my outfit a bit of a turn on.

Vicky (*laughing*) I do, I do.

Andrew Well then, I'm determined that we walk as slowly as we can so that I can keep it on as long as possible. With any luck you'll be in a positive frenzy of lust for me by the time we get back to the hotel.

Vicky I think I'm in a bit of a frenzy for you right now actually.

Andrew Really?

Vicky Really! (*She gives him a kiss*) Very nice. And you are such a good kisser! Perhaps we should start walking a bit faster. I want to bagsie the double bed for us.

Andrew Steady on, I don't think there's any chance of hot sex in those family rooms we're all sharing.

Vicky I know that, but it will drive Yvonne absolutely mad if we just sleep in the same bed, and I can't resist it!

Andrew Look, I know I agreed with you to act like a bit of a prat on the train for a laugh and to wind Yvonne up, but I can't let the girls all go home still thinking badly of me. So let's drop the teasing when we get back to the hotel, shall we? It'll be nice to stop the act and just be me again!

Vicky Spoilsport! Oh all right then!

Andrew Thanks.

Vicky Oh — look out — one of your laces is undone ...

Andrew kneels and ties his lace. Short pause as Vicky considers what to say

Before we see the others ...

Andrew (*standing*) Yes?

Vicky Well, when I read your card on the train it was a real shock, I wouldn't have pressed you to come if I'd known ... why didn't you tell me?

Andrew (*sighing*) It's just so hard to tell people something like that, especially if you don't know them very well. I wanted to tell you, but I didn't know how you would react. I didn't want you to go out with me because you pitied me ... and I really wanted to come on the walk when Chloe dropped out. It sounded like it would be a good laugh. You don't, do you?

Vicky What?

Andrew Pity me.

Vicky No. I don't pity you, don't ever think that. Quite the opposite ...

They hug each other, and stroll off arm in arm

Black-out

9 miles into the walk

The Lights snap up on Madge and Ethel, cockney old dears. In the ensemble version of Act III, Ethel may be substituted by a male actor playing Madge's husband, Ron. They are race marshalls. Ethel/Ron is solemnly holding a placard with "9 miles" on it. Madge is shouting encouragement to the masses of walkers. They wear huge fluorescent jackets and woolly hats, scarves and gloves

Madge (*excited*) Oh it's marvellous to be doing our bit, isn't it, Ethel? I'm so glad we volunteered to be marshalls tonight. I really feel part of it all. At my age I can just about make it up the stairs in one piece, never mind do a midnight walk, but this is brilliant! I mean, I might be one boob short and full of rheumatism but there's nothing wrong with me vocal chords ... (*Shouting to the unseen crowds of walkers*) Come on now, girls, you can do it, you can do it. That's it, keep your spirits up, keep moving, there we go.

Ethel (*slightly jealous of Madge's leading role*) Haven't you got a sore throat by now, Madge? Do you know, I couldn't keep up all that shouting like that.

Madge No, I know *you* couldn't, Ethel, but that's why *you've* got the placard, isn't it? You've got stronger arms than me, and *I've* got ...

Ethel (*under her breath*) A big mouth ...

Madge ... and *I've* got —— What did you say, Ethel?

Ethel (*shouting up*) I said you've got a good loud voice, Madge.

Madge Yes, yes ... and we both agreed that that was what was needed for my role. A loud voice and an enthusiastic personality, you know — the ability to motivate people ...

Ethel (*in a slightly peeved tone of voice*) I know, I know ... but my arms are starting to hurt now. It's quite heavy this placard, you know, heavier than it looks.

Madge (*shouting to the walking masses*) That's it, ladies, you've done nine miles now, well done. All for charity, remember, keep going ... Keep going ... What did you say, Ethel?

Ethel I said my arms are starting to hurt a bit. These placards are heavier than they look ...

Madge Well, why didn't you do those exercises like I told you to, you know, with the baked bean tins?

Ethel looks at Madge blankly

(*Carefully explaining*) You know, you take a tin of baked beans in each hand and you hold your arms out at the sides like this. (*She holds an imaginary tin in each hand and lifts her arms slowly up at each side until each arm is held out directly at shoulder level*) And you hold for ten seconds. (*She pedantically counts down from ten*) Ten, nine, eight, seven, six ...

Ethel (*interrupting and finishing the countdown very quickly for her*) Five, four, three, two, one!

Madge glares at her and continues with her instructions

Madge And then you lower the tins slowly to your sides and you repeat as often as you can ... it's very easy ... no gym to go to ... you can do it while you're waiting for the kettle to boil ... and it's very good for toning your upper arms!

Ethel (*solemnly*) But I don't like baked beans!

Madge (*impatiently*) Well it doesn't have to be baked beans, does it? You can do it with tinned spaghetti, tomatoes — any tin really — tinned peas — you like peas, don't you?

Ethel I prefer frozen ones myself actually ...

They are just about to discuss the merits of frozen versus tinned peas when there is the loud sound of a man's voice over a walkie talkie radio. Madge has forgotten her walkie talkie is in her pocket and she looks suitably startled and looks around

Radio Voice Hello, hello ... Can you read me?

Madge Who's that ...

Ethel (*solemnly*) In your pocket ...

Radio Voice (*in an official tone of voice*) Hello, hello — can you hear me?

Madge (*shouting into the night*) Yes — we can hear you.

Radio Voice (*in an exasperated tone*) Hello, hello! Typical, the stupid bloody woman hasn't got her radio turned on.

Ethel (*in a bored tone*) Madge, it's in your pocket

Madge Oh God — yes! (*She scrabbles around in her pocket for it and holds it reverentially to her ear*)

Radio Voice This is base to point number nine. Hello, hello. Would the marshalls at the nine mile point come in please?

Madge (*slowly in her official radio voice*) This is Madge to base, Madge to base. Do you read me?

Radio Voice (*loudly*) Hello! Hello! Can you hear me?

Madge (*louder and slower official voice*) Point number nine to base. I read you loud and clear. Do you read me?

Ethel (*in a bored tone*) You have to push it in.

Madge What?

~~Ethel~~ The button on the side of the radio. You have to push it in when you speak so they can hear you.

Radio Voice (*exasperated*) Push in the button on the side of the bloody ——

Madge (*forcefully pushing in the button; interrupting*) This is Madge to base, Madge to base, do you read me?

Radio Voice About time! Is everything OK at your point? We're just checking in case you need anything.

Madge (*emphatically pushing in the button again*) All in order here, sir. Don't worry about us two, point number nine is fully functional.

Radio Voice Well if you need anything just give me a shout, OK? Over and out.

Madge Will do. (*She goes to put the radio in her pocket and hurriedly holds it to her mouth again and says loudly in her best official voice*) Roger, and over and out. (*She puts the radio carefully back in her pocket*)

~~Ethel~~ Can I have a go next time? I've always wanted to say that.

Madge Course you can, course you can. Oh look, here's some of the girls again. (*Shouting*) Come on, you girls, you can do it. You're doing really well now, girls, keep putting those feet down, one step at a time remember ...

Vicky and Andrew stroll on arm in arm

Madge's verbal encouragement for the walkers is momentarily frozen as she cannot quite decide how to encourage what she thinks are two women in love who are not afraid to show it

Come on now, girls, keep it going, nine miles down so you're doing really well.

Andrew and Vicky stroll past Madge

Vicky (*shouting over to Madge*) We are doing well, aren't we, and do you know what?

Madge (*slightly unsure of the situation but desperately trying to appear politically correct*) What's that, dear?

Vicky (*looking at Andrew*) I think I might be in love!!

Madge (*looking over her shoulder at Ethel with a "Help me" look on her face — then back to Vicky*) Well ... that's marvellous, love, absolutely marvellous ... really wonderful ...

Andrew gently cups Vicky's face in his hands and kisses her tenderly. Madge desperately tries to draw Ethel's attention to the situation. Ethel is looking the other way, a bored expression on her face

Andrew and Vicky stroll off arm in arm

Madge stares after them in shocked silence. Slight pause

Ethel (*loudly and sulkily breaking the silence*) My arms are still hurting
  you know ...
Madge (*in a shocked tone*) Did you see that?
Ethel What?
Madge Those two girls kissing, and in broad daylight!
Ethel It's hardly broad daylight is it? It's the middle of the night.
Madge You know what I mean. Well, I never!

Ethel has hidden depths

Ethel True love knows no boundaries, Madge, no boundaries. Come on
  now, you were around in the sixties. (*Gently, she sings a few words of
  "All You Need Is Love"*) — and all that. Don't be so narrow-minded!
Madge Yes, I suppose you're right. But ... well ... I never. You don't see
  a lot of girls kissing like that on our estate.
Ethel (*handing the placard to Madge*) Well, while you're struck dumb
  you can hold this placard and I'll have a go at the shouting lark.

*Ethel seizes the chance to step forward and take centre stage. Her
demeanour changes from bored sidekick to born performer*

  (*Clapping her hands and changing the encouragement style to a loud
  football chant*) Moonwalk! Moonwalk! Come on, you Moonwalkers!
  Come on now, come on, everyone ...

*Ethel pointedly looks over her shoulder at Madge. Madge is still in a
state of shock*

  ... of all sexes and sexual preferences, shift those feet. Just keep
  thinking of how much money you'll raise and how many lives you're
  going to help, that's it — (*She sings "Keep Right on to the End of the
  Road" in a comic vein as she marches across the stage*) That's the
  spirit, well done, well done.

*Sounds of the crowd. Pause. Ethel looks happily on at the walking
masses*

Madge Ethel?
Ethel (*still encouraging the unseen masses*) Yes, Madge.

Madge (*shamefacedly*) I've been thinking. I need to think before I speak really.

~~**Ethel**~~ Don't worry about it, we all make mistakes.

Madge No, no, credit where it's due, you were right you know! (*After a ponderous pause*) This placard is a lot heavier than it looks!

Black-out

SCENE 8

11 miles into the race

There should be a pantomime feel to this scene. The Handsome Drunk can double up with the Policeman or a Marshall in the ensemble version, and with Andrew in the version for a cast of 6

The Lights come up and Handsome Drunk, a tipsy, good-looking guy enters. He is dressed in a dinner suit and black tie, a half-drunk bottle of champagne held nonchalantly in one hand, his jacket slung over his shoulder, his tie undone. He bears an uncanny resemblance to Andrew but has dark hair instead of blonde ... He is on his way home from a good night out at a formal function of some kind. He is humming a tune from "My Fair Lady" as he enters — the song is "On The Street Where You Live". He takes a few unsteady dance steps as he hums before bursting into song with the assured abandon of a jolly drunk. He has a good voice, but slurs his words a bit and the timing etc. is definitely out

He sings the first line, ideally fixing his eye on a female in the audience as he does so. He stumbles slightly under the influence of the champagne and chuckles to himself

He sings the next three lines, then does an almighty burp, stops and takes a dramatic swig from the bottle

> *Yvonne and Maggie enter unseen by Handsome Drunk, and stop, and then stare at him. Yvonne is still limping slightly and holding the wand limply in her hand*

Handsome Drunk does not see them. He bursts loudly into song again, his eyes closed. He hugs the champagne bottle to his chest. He continues the song, then pauses. He continues again, then pauses again. Yvonne and Maggie continue to stare open-mouthed at him

Handsome Drunk continues. He is still unaware of Yvonne and Maggie. He sings the next few lines very softly and romantically, getting quieter and quieter ...

Slight pause. He grins inanely at whoever he has fixed his eye on in the audience — enough of a pause for the audience to just about think he has stopped singing when ... still unaware of the girls — he throws his arms wide and belts the next lines out very loudly. The girls jump slightly like frightened schoolgirls but are still entranced ...

He spins around with his imaginary dance partner and is now facing the girls as he sings the next words

He opens his eyes. The girls simper — an unexpected sight for sore eyes — a slight pause

Handsome Drunk (*appreciatively*) Wow — look at you!

The girls giggle like teenagers meeting a pop idol. Handsome Drunk returns to the song, serenading the girls for a few lines. He kneels before them and sings the next line very quietly again

He bows his head — they think he has finished and step forward to applaud when he lifts his head and belts out the next line very loudly ... They jump back again nervously and giggle

He bows his head again in a mock theatrical gesture — the girls break into enthusiastic applause

Maggie I've never been serenaded before.
Yvonne I feel like a princess!
Handsome Drunk And may I say you look like a princess. (*He continues in a mock-theatrical manner. He is all man*)

Maggie and Yvonne are enchanted

What divine costumes you are wearing, ladies, and all matching too! Let me guess, are you in the chorus line of a West End show?
Yvonne (*entranced*) No such luck, I'm afraid.
Maggie We're walking the Moonwalk.
Handsome Drunk "The Moonwalk". Sounds like a truly celestial event. How far have you come?
Maggie About eleven miles so far, we're doing the half marathon so we've only got a couple of miles to go now.

Yvonne It's to raise money for a breast cancer charity.

Handsome Drunk (*with sincere admiration*) Well done, well done. Well — that of course explains the wonderful display of your womanly charms, does it not?

The girls' bosoms rise visibly in response as he says this

May I say that you are a veritable feast for this man's eyes. (*He bows again theatrically*)

The girls are now his menopausal groupies. Yvonne is very taken with him and responds with a theatrical curtsy

Yvonne Why, thank you, kind sir.

Handsome Drunk May I walk with you a while, young maidens? I live not half a mile hence.

Yvonne (*enthusiastically*) Why of course, of course. (*She limps towards him*)

Handsome Drunk Why, dear maiden, you are in pain ... (*He kneels at Yvonne's feet*) 'Tis your slipper, is it not? Has it rubbed your heel on the long journey?

There is the loud sound effect of fairy dust. Yvonne stares down at him, enraptured. Handsome Drunk holds her foot gently to examine her heel. The wand which she has been holding limply in her hand now rises visibly

Yvonne Oh, I feel just like Cinderella with Prince Charming!

Maggie (*aside to the audience; grumpily folding her arms*) No prizes for guessing who the ugly sister is tonight then!

Handsome Drunk (*oblivious to this comment; rising unsteadily to his feet*) I have observed a slight chill, my lady, and would wish to protect your fair skin from the vagaries of the night air. May I offer you my cloak for your protection? (*He goes to place his jacket round Yvonne's shoulders*)

Yvonne is positively swooning by now

Maggie (*stepping forward to try and get in on the act*) Actually I'm feeling the cold awfully myself tonight.

Yvonne (*hissing an aside to her*) Back off, this one's mine.

Maggie backs off a few paces looking a bit miffed, leaving Yvonne and Handsome Drunk c. Yvonne smiles sweetly at him. He gallantly places his coat round her shoulders

Why thank you, kind sir.

Handsome Drunk offers his arm to Yvonne. She takes it in a genteel fashion. He takes another swig from the champagne bottle, smiles sweetly at her and loudly hiccups

Handsome Drunk (*with exaggerated fondness*) Would you care to stroll up the avenue then, my lady?
Yvonne I most certainly would, my lord.

Maggie looks duly neglected and isolated, enough so as to elicit a sympathetic "aah" from the audience. Handsome Drunk unexpectedly turns to the disconsolate Maggie and offers her his other arm

Handsome Drunk Do you know, I've always dreamed of walking through London with a beautiful woman on each arm. Would you care to make my dream come true?

Another sound of fairy dust is heard. Maggie perks up, curtsies, and takes his arm and looks up at him

Original version:	*Ensemble version*:
Maggie Why thank you, I'd love to. Do you know, you look vaguely familiar and I can't think why. Have you got any brothers at all? **Handsome Drunk** None that I can recall, but then again my father was well travelled and a bit of a rogue so you never know. **Yvonne** You're right, you know, Maggie, he reminds me of someone as well. (*She stares at him*) Can't think who for now but it'll come to me. **Handsome Drunk** Ready, ladies?	**Maggie** Why thank you. I'd love to! **Handsome Drunk** Ready ladies?

They exit arm in arm, Yvonne still limping. Handsome Drunk bursts into song again and the girls join in enthusiastically as they go

Black-out

In the black-out the sound of heavy traffic fades up as the next scene comes into view

SCENE 9

12 miles into the walk

A "12 miles" placard stands C. *In the ensemble version of the act, Marshall 5 holds the placard. A Policeman's whistle is heard, then his voice (recorded or from a microphone off stage) as he directs the traffic. In the ensemble version, the Policeman may appear on stage with a whistle*

Policeman Sorry, folks, it's a bit dangerous here so we'll have to wait for a gap in the traffic before I can let you across ... This is a busy road.

An impatient driver beeps his horn

Keep your hair on, sir — they'll all be across shortly.

There is the sound of a car screeching away impatiently

I've made a note of your number, matey ... I've made a note of it.

Hilary and Siobhan enter at a fast pace

They slow to a halt as they realize that they have to wait for another gap in the traffic. They look over towards the Policeman (either unseen or on stage) and the traffic

Hilary Christ, we'll have to wait for the long arm of the law to stop the traffic again ... (*Checking her watch*) Mind you, we're ahead of our target time!! Look at that. (*She enthusiastically shows Siobhan her watch*) That's brilliant!
Siobhan That's great, Hilary, I'm so pleased for you.
Hilary That's really bucked me up. I was definitely feeling the pace just then. Let's murder the last mile! (*Impatiently watching the traffic*) Come on, come on — wouldn't you think that policeman would just stop the traffic and let us through ...
Siobhan Hilary, Hilary!

Hilary does not hear her. She is busy looking for a gap in the traffic

Policeman OK, ladies, there's a nice gap in the traffic now so let's get you all across while we can ...

The Policeman's whistle is heard. The sound of cars halting

Come on, folks — all of you, quick as you can now ...

Hilary Come on, Siobhan! He's stopped the traffic. We'll have to get moving if we want to get that personal best in.

Siobhan (*hanging back*) Listen, Hilary, you go on ahead. It's only a little way to go now, and I know how important it is to you to finish with a fast time.

Hilary (*confused*) What do you mean "go on ahead"? Are you all right? You haven't hurt your foot as well have you?

Siobhan No, no, it's not that.

Hilary (*getting ratty*) Well what the hell is it? Come on, Siobhan, we haven't got time for a girly chat now. We've trained really hard for tonight and ...

Siobhan I know, I know ... (*Hesitantly*) But ... I want to go back.

Hilary (*astounded*) You want to go back? Did I hear you right? You want to go back?

Siobhan (*bravely*) Yes, I do!

Hilary Why on earth do you want to go back, we've nearly finished!

Siobhan For the others ... I want to find them so we can all finish together.

Policeman Right, girls — you'll have to wait now. I can't hold this traffic up all night for you ...

Sound of traffic starting again

Hilary The others are all right, and we're on target for a personal best, remember. Come on ...

Siobhan Don't mind me. You go on without me. It's the final mile now ... I'll see you at the finish line. (*She turns to walk away*)

Hilary (*grabbing Siobhan's arm*) Hey, hold on. What's this all about, Siobhan? I don't get it.

Siobhan (*standing her ground, disengaging herself from Hilary's grasp*) Look, I know you want to do a personal best, and that it means a lot to you, but this is my night as well, and it's more important to me that we all cross the finishing line together. Tonight's not all about fast times, Hilary, not for me anyway.

Hilary (*in a manic tone*) But we'll all meet up again at the finish line. We all agreed, remember, we all agreed when Yvonne hurt her foot.

Siobhan (*interrupting*) I know, I know. But it won't be the same, will it? I just feel that if we all finish together, you know ... It'll be how we all wanted it to be ... a team, and we'll be just like one big happy ... (*She stops herself finishing the sentence, feeling awkward*)

Hilary (*slowly finishing it for her*) ... like one big happy family ...

There is a long pause. Hilary breaks the moment

I'm sorry, Siobhan ... sorry. I didn't realize how much that meant to you.

Siobhan You go on ahead, it's OK ... really.

Hilary No, no. God, I can't believe that I made you leave the others behind like that ... I just wanted to do a personal best ... for my mum ... I wanted her to know I'd tried really hard ...

Siobhan Hilary, you don't have to prove anything to anyone — we all know how much you loved her ...

Long pause while Hilary makes her decision

Hilary I never thought I'd ever say this to anyone, but do you fancy walking backwards for a few miles then?

Siobhan (*smiling*) Think you can keep up with me? I'm good, you know. I bet I'm the first one to spot the others.

Hilary's competitive nature returns and she strikes a pose to retrace their steps as though she is at the start of the 100 metres dash

Hilary The last one to spot them buys the ale later on tonight! (*Speeding off*) And they're off! Come on, Cheshire Cats, let's go ...

Siobhan (*shaking her head*) Bloody cheat! (*Shouting after Hilary as she follows her*) Remember — walk, don't run!

Hilary and Siobhan exit

Policeman (*shouting*) Ladies, ladies, you're going the wrong way!

Original version:	*Ensemble version:*
Policeman (*with a big sigh*) Well, I've always thought women had a strange sense of direction, but that takes the flaming biscuit!	**Marshall 5** Well, I've always thought women had a strange sense of direction, but that takes the flaming biscuit!

*In the original version of the act, traffic noises are heard, followed by a
Black-out to indicate the end of the scene*

The following may be added for the ensemble version of the act:

*Marshall 5 contentedly sips at a cup of tea he has poured himself from a
flask in his pocket. Policeman looks on enviously*

Policeman (*to Marshall 5*) They're all in a hurry tonight, aren't they?
(*He rubs his hands together*) God, it's cold tonight. Absolutely
freezing! (*He looks at the flask pointedly — slight pause*) Is that tea
you've got there?
Marshall 5 (*sipping appreciatively and noisily*) Yes.

Another slight pause. Policeman eyes the tea

Policeman (*enviously*) Bet that's warming you up a treat ... eh ... a nice
hot cuppa ... Can't beat it, can you ...?

Another slight pause. Policeman looks on. No cuppa is forthcoming

Marshall 5 (*sipping the tea appreciatively*) Yes ...

*Another pause. Policeman makes a laboured point of stamping his feet and
rubbing his hand together in the cold night air in the hope of a free cuppa*

(*Philosophically*) Weak but sweet ...
Policeman Who is?
Marshall 5 The tea ... that's how I like it ...

Pause. Marshall 5 continues to drink his tea

Policeman (*eventually pleading*) You couldn't spare a drop, could you?
I'm flaming gasping here!
Marshall 5 (*pedantically*) Well, will it be OK for you? Some folk don't
like it sweet ... some don't like it weak ...
Policeman (*exasperated*) I'll take what I can bloody get ...
Marshall 5 (*handing over the cup and flask to the Policeman*) I'll just
nip over the road to the car and get a cup for you — hold that for me
— back in a tick ...

Marshall 5 trots off

Policeman (*shouting after Marshall 5*) Mind that traffic now ...

There are squeals of brakes. Busy traffic noise again. Policeman, now all smiles, quietly strolls centre stage. Then there is a huge squeal of breaks and the sound of a crash. Policeman looks across, looks back at the audience, shrugs his shoulders, tastes the tea and drinks it ... smacking his lips appreciatively ...

Black-out

SCENE 10

The end of the Walk

The Lights come up gradually and fill the stage with a soft pink glow. There is a large banner aloft that states "Finish"

The "Chariots of Fire" music fades up also and plays throughout what should be a slightly surreal sequence with no dialogue. The team enters slowly one by one down the exit funnel, foil capes round their shoulders, in the following order: Yvonne, Maggie, Vicky, Andrew, Siobhan, Hilary

In the ensemble version of the act a Photographer and Marshalls enter and note the girls' race numbers, hand out foil capes, put medals on them, and take a photo of each individual team member before the group photograph at the end of the sequence. The Photographer treats the audience as race participants by also taking pictures of them during this scene

They excitedly show each other their medals. Andrew sweeps Vicky up in his arms and gallantly carries her over to the others like a groom carrying a bride over the threshold. Laughter from all and hugs all round. All shuffle into position for a team photo — they all kiss their medals and look happy and wave as the picture is taken

There is a big flash from a camera and the sound effect of crowd cheers

Sudden Black-out

ACT IV — RETURNING

Chester Railway Station

There is a platform sign for Chester and a station bench on stage. In the black-out the sound of a busy railway station is heard. A train is heard pulling into the station, and people emerging and bustling down the platforms

Still in the black-out the bored tone of the station announcer is heard as well. His diction is still poor

Announcer The train now arriving at Platform ... (*His voice fades out*) ... will be calling at ... (*His voice fades out*) ... and ... (*His voice fades out*) ... Passengers travelling to ... (*His voice fades out*) ... in order to catch their connection, must ensure that they alight at ... (*His voice fades out*) ... I repeat, *must* ensure that they alight at ... (*His voice fades out*) ... John, I am still waiting for that ten pounds, you sore loser, you — still waiting.

The Lights come up on the girls and Andrew having just alighted from the train and carrying their bags — some are taking a picture of the others: much bonhomie and jollity. They are partly dressed in their walking strip, coats thrown over the top etc., medals round some of their necks, indicating a good party was had the previous night and there was a rush to Euston station the next day to catch the train

Yvonne (*referring to the announcer*) God help anyone who has to change trains!

Andrew and Vicky stand arm in arm

Vicky I am absolutely whacked! And I've got a terrible crick in my neck.
Andrew Same here.
Siobhan You two were a sight for sore eyes on that train, fast asleep and with your arms round each other all the way.
Vicky And we were arm in arm all the way round on the walk last night. It was lovely to have that support from Andrew. My feet were

absolutely killing me! (*To Andrew seductively*) You can give me a foot massage later tonight, darling.

Andrew Can't wait, Twinkle Toes! Shall we make a move then?

Vicky (*turning to the others*) Bye, girls, we're off to get a taxi. See you soon, it was a great weekend!

Andrew and Vicky rush off hand in hand

Hilary, Yvonne, Siobhan and Maggie wave them off. They shout jolly goodbyes etc. which change to a loud groan as soon as the couple are out of sight

Hilary (*staring after them*) I'd hate to be their taxi driver. Andrew will probably start sucking her toes as soon as they hit that back seat.

Yvonne Yeah, and sharing that family room with them was a bit of a nightmare last night ... well ... until I made him sleep in the bath at any rate.

Siobhan Less of that, you two. Just remember how much he's raised in sponsorship money.

Hilary God, yes! Five hundred pounds! That's brought our team total to over two grand. I'm so proud of you all! Come on, group hug, group hug. What a team, what a team!!

They all do the Cheshire Cats group hug, a big miaow, and end up laughing at each other. Magie sits down again on the bench while the others stand and chat. While they chat she quietly takes out the cards they all wrote on the train down and reads them to herself

Siobhan Right, girls. Time for the ride home. My feet can't take much more standing around. Those London pavements were so hard last night!

Yvonne I'm going to have a long hot soak in the tub tonight.

Siobhan And a dream about lover boy!

Yvonne Now stop that, you're only jealous. And besides, it was all very innocent as you well know. Maggie can back me up on that.

Maggie He was a bit of a charmer though, wasn't he, Yvonne?

Yvonne Just a bit.

Siobhan Just a bit! Hilary and I were bloody green when we found you both strolling along with that hunk. I'd have definitely found an opportunity to take advantage of him along the way.

Yvonne It wasn't like that at all. It was just a lot of innocent flirting. He was an absolute gentleman. (*She smiles to herself as she recalls*) Yes ... a proper Prince Charming. It was lovely to see that the age of

chivalry is not completely dead ... And then you two sods turned up
and scared him off!

Hilary I thought you were pleased to see us.

Yvonne I'm only kidding. I was made up you came back for me and
Maggie. It was a great feeling finishing all together like that.

Siobhan notices that Maggie is reading the cards, and sits beside her

Siobhan Are those the cards we all wrote on the way down to London,
Maggie?

Maggie Yes. I was just reminding myself why we did the walk in the
first place. I haven't had a chance to look at them properly till now.

Yvonne (*nosily sitting by Maggie*) Are we allowed to have a peek or are
they purely to be used for artistic purposes for your exhibition?

Maggie looks slightly uncomfortable

(*Persisting*) Well, can we have a peek or not?

Maggie They're quite personal really. I know you'll all see them if you
come to see my exhibition in June, but if you see them before then —
well — I'd feel like I was breaking a confidence in a way.

Yvonne (*hacked off*) Oh, OK then!

Hilary Yvonne, leave her alone you nosy thing.

Yvonne But they must be really interesting reading though.

Maggie (*earnestly*) Yes, they are ... one of them in particular ... (*She is
beginning to weaken*)

Siobhan Oh now, come on, Maggie. We all knew they were going to
be for public display, it's not like they're a secret is it? (*She sits on the
other side of Maggie on the bench*)

Hilary stands behind looking over their shoulders

Maggie Well, I suppose not ...

Hilary Ah ha! She's starting to crack! Come on then, let's see this one
card then, the one you mentioned — just that one.

Siobhan
Yvonne } (*together*) Ah, go on, go on, go on, go on, go on, go on, go on ...

Maggie (*relenting*) Only if you promise not to talk about it to anyone
else!

Yvonne
Siobhan } (*together*) We promise!

Maggie OK then ... (*She holds the card up in the middle of the little
group*)

Yvonne, Siobhan and Hilary ad-lib intially: "Let's see", "Hold it straight," "It's written in capitals", "Lovely handwriting" etc. They fall silent as they read the card. The atmosphere changes from schoolgirl teasing and jollity to a serious, almost shocked feeling. There is absolute silence and stillness for a few moments

Yvonne (*blurting out*) But I thought Andrew was divorced.
Siobhan (*holding the card and slowly reading it*) So did I. Let's face it, we all did, but the truth is that he did that walk in memory of her ... his wife ...
Hilary She must have been so young ...
Yvonne (*guilt-ridden*) I feel terrible, all those comments I made about him. Oh my God! And the things I said to his face as well.
Hilary Does Vicky know?
Maggie She must know, they were both reading each other's cards when I collected them from you all on the train.
Siobhan (*puzzled*) But I don't understand ... all weekend. They were both so ...
Maggie Happy?
Siobhan Yes ... happy.

There is an almost childlike sincerity about Maggie at this point

Maggie Well that's how I feel. That's how we all felt in the end didn't we? Happy that we all did the walk together.
Yvonne ⎫
Siobhan ⎭ (*together; displaying their medals*) And proud!
Hilary And knackered?
Maggie (*laughing*) That as well. But it was a great night! (*She puts the cards back in her bag*)
Yvonne I couldn't have done it without you, Maggie. You were so good to stick with me, you and your never-ending supply of padded plasters.
Siobhan She's such a practical little soul underneath that arty farty exterior.
Maggie Hey, less of the arty farty, you!
Hilary Come on, folks, I'm fading fast here. I've got to get home to my bed. Last one to the taxi rank's a sissy, but remember ...
Yvonne ⎫
Maggie ⎬ (*together; shouting*) Walk — don't run!
Siobhan ⎭

Siobhan, Hilary and Yvonne pick up their bags. Maggie hangs back

Maggie My husband is picking me up, girls. I'd offer you a lift but he's bringing the kids so I can't fit you all in the car.

Hilary That's OK. I bet the kids are dying to see you. You can show off your medal to them. Do you want us to wait with you?

Maggie No, no ... you all go on, it's OK.

Yvonne (*hugging Maggie*) Listen, my trusty little walking companion, give me a buzz when your art exhibition is due on. We all want to come and see it.

Maggie I will, I will.

Siobhan Yes, and we'll all have an opportunity to apologize to Andrew if he's there with Vicky.

Hilary You're right, but I'm sure he's not the type to hold a grudge.

Yvonne No chance, he's too busy holding Vicky's erogenous zones.

Siobhan (*to Yvonne and Hilary*) Right, girls, are we off then?

After lots of hugs and goodbyes, Hilary, Siobhan and Yvonne leave the stage arm in arm, waving to Maggie as they go

Maggie stands c, *waving them off and smiling*

The sound of a train departing from the station grows louder and louder, reaching a climax and then there is a sudden momentary black-out and silence. A spotlight comes up on Maggie sitting alone on the bench. She speaks directly to the audience

Maggie Andrew's card was a surprise to all of us. And it touched a few hearts when I held my art exhibition. (*She searches for the words*) So many of our friends and relations had been affected by cancer, some more than others ... (*Pause*) ... I just couldn't tell the girls that weekend that I had to go for some tests the following week ... I didn't want to spoil all the fun, and it made me want to do the walk even more ... (*Long pause as she struggles to continue. She speaks in verse*)

> One day we're ordinary people living ordinary lives,
> Then we lose someone who's dear to us
> — a friend, a child, a wife —
> And we wonder if we'll ever find
> The strength to carry on
> Without that special someone,
> Without that special bond.
> But that night we all felt strong enough
> To join a great big band
> Of people who decided
> To come out and make a stand

And show that it's not good enough
If we just talk the talk
We should go one step further,
And we should walk the Walk.
We found our strength in numbers ...
We really found our feet
When we all walked out together
And we finally hit the streets.
You know ... folk are just amazing
When they decide to give
At one time and all together —
To help someone to live ...

(*After a pause*) The girls are all walking again this year, and this time ... they're doing it for me. (*She gazes out into the distance over the audience*)

We hear Maggie's pre-recorded voice fade up to echo slowly and softly a softer version of the Cheshire Cats marching song. As her voice fades up in volume the spot on Maggie's face slowly fades out by the end of this sequence

Maggie's Voice   I don't know but I've been told,
Cheshire Cats are good as gold.
They pump their muscles, hit their stride
It makes them feel real good inside.

We hear her voice gently echoing in the darkness

Slight pause, a few seconds' silence, then music and lights full on for the curtain call which should be very jolly to lift the mood again before the audience leave

At the end of the curtain call the photographer (in the ensemble version) or Andrew ushers the cast around the bench for a group photograph. They all smile. He spins on his heel, gesturing to the audience to smile as well, and takes a photo of them. There is a huge flash of the camera

Black-out

CURTAIN

FURNITURE AND PROPERTY LIST

ACT I

On stage: Row of four pink chairs

Personal: **Vicky**: bumbag containing cat's tail, ears and long slinky black gloves
Maggie: bumbag containing plasters
Hilary: watch, bumbag containing local maps, small book and pen

ACT II
SCENE 1

Set: Second row of four pink chairs

Off stage: Weekend bag, handbag, train tickets, bottle of water, energy bar **(Hilary)**
Weekend bag, handbag, magazine **(Siobhan)**
Bags containing Jenga, pens and postcards, magazines, food for the train **(Maggie)**
Bags, magazines, food for the train **(Yvonne)**
Small overnight bag **(Andrew)**

SCENE 2

Set: Rearrange chairs as described in stage directions
Arrange bags and their contents as described in stage directions

ACT III

SCENE 1

Strike: Chairs, bags and their contents

SCENE 2

Off stage: Whistle **(Aerobics Instructor)**
Food in foil tray, small camera **(Siobhan)**
Food in foil tray, huge bottle of water **(Hilary)**
Food in foil tray, bag for rubbish **(Maggie)**
Food in foil tray **(Yvonne)**

Personal: **Hilary**: watch, bumbag
                 Siobhan: bumbag
                 Maggie: bumbag containing plasters
                 Andrew: pink Barbie backpack

Scene 3

Set: "Start" banner

Off stage: Large flashing fairy wand (**Hilary**)

Scene 4

Strike: "Start" banner

Set: Sign saying "5 mile mark"
                 Crates of bottled water

Scene 5

Strike: Sign saying "5 mile mark"
                 Crates of bottled water

Scene 6

Off stage: Placard with "9 miles" on it (**Ethel/Ron**)
                 Walkie talkie (**Madge**)

Scene 7

Off stage: Half-drunk bottle of champagne (**Handsome Drunk**)

Scene 8

Set: "12 miles" placard

Off stage: Flask of tea (**Marshall 5** in ensemble version)
                 Whistle (**Policeman** in ensemble version)

Scene 9

Strike: "12 miles" placard

Set: "Finish" banner

Off stage: Medals, foil capes (**Yvonne**, **Maggie**, **Vicky**, **Andrew**,
                 Siobhan, **Hilary**)

ACT IV

Strike: "Finish" banner

Set: Platform sign for Chester
              Station bench

Off stage: Bags, medals, camera (**Yvonne**, **Maggie**, **Vicky**, **Andrew**,
                 Siobhan, **Hilary**)
              Card (**Maggie**)

LIGHTING PLOT

Property fittings required: nil

ACT I

To open: General exterior lighting

Cue 1	**Vicky**: "And there he was." *Spotlight on side of stage where* **Andrew** *will enter*	(Page 14)
Cue 2	**Vicky** growls to herself *Lights snap back up*	(Page 16)
Cue 3	**Maggie** leaves *Lights fade out*	(Page 22)

ACT II, SCENE 1

To open: General exterior lighting

| *Cue* 4 | Sound of a train approaching and stopping
Lights slowly start to fade down to black-out | (Page 33) |

ACT II, SCENE 2

To open: Interior lighting for a train

| *Cue* 5 | Sound of train reaches a climax
Black-out | (Page 41) |

ACT III, SCENE 1

To open: Spotlight on Hilary

| *Cue* 6 | **Hilary**: "London's streets, here we come!"
Black-out | (Page 43) |

ACT III, SCENE 2

To open: Darkness

Cue 7	**Aerobics Instructor** blows his/her whistle	(Page 43)
	Bright coloured lights snap up	
Cue 8	**Hilary** leads them all out, chanting	(Page 50)
	Black-out	

ACT III, Scene 3

To open: General night time exterior lighting

Cue 9	**Girls** and **Andrew** exit [Original version]/	(Page 54)
	Marshall 1 and **Marshall 2** exit	(Page 55)
	[Ensemble version]	
	Black-out	

ACT III, Scene 4

To open: General night time exterior lighting

Cue 10	**Maggie** and **Yvonne** exit laughing	(Page 58)
	Black-out	

ACT III, Scene 5

To open: General night time exterior lighting

Cue 10	**Hilary/Marshall 4**: " ... with global warming??"	(Page 62)
	Black-out	

ACT III, Scene 6

To open: General night time exterior lighting

Cue 11	**Vicky** and **Andrew** stroll off arm in arm	(Page 63)
	Black-out	

ACT III, Scene 7

To open: General night time exterior lighting

Cue 12	**Madge**: "... a lot heavier than it looks!"	(Page 68)
	Black-out	

ACT III, Scene 8

To open: General night time exterior lighting

Cue 13   **Maggie, Yvonne** and **Handsome Drunk** exit   (Page 71)
                Black-out

ACT III, SCENE 9

To open: General night time exterior lighting

Cue 14   **Policeman's Voice**: "... that takes the flaming
                    biscuit!" [Original version]   (Page 74)
                Policeman smacks his lips appreciatively
                    [Ensemble version]   (Page 76)
                Black-out

ACT III, SCENE 10

To open: Lights come up gradually and fill the room with a soft pink glow

Cue 15   Big flash from the camera and crowd cheers   (Page 76)
                Sudden black-out

ACT IV

To open: Darkness

Cue 16   **Announcer**: " — still waiting."   (Page 77)
                Bring up Lights

Cue 17   Sound of train departing reaches a climax   (Page 81)
                Sudden momentary black-out, then spotlight on **Maggie**

Cue 18   **Maggie's Voice** fades up in volume   (Page 82)
                Spotlight fades slowly to black-out

Cue 19   **Maggie's Voice** gently echoes, followed   (Page 82)
                    by a slight pause and a few seconds' silence
                Bring up Lights

Cue 20   Big flash of the camera   (Page 82)
                Black-out

EFFECTS PLOT

ACT I

Cue 1   To open ACT I   (Page 1)
Traffic noise and birdsong can be heard

Cue 2   **Hilary**: "Here for your approval is Vicky's design."   (Page 12)
Stripper theme tune plays

Cue 3   **Vicky**: "And there he was."   (Page 14)
Sound of christening party

Cue 4   **Vicky** growls to herself   (Page 16)
Cut sound of christening party

Cue 5   Lights fade out   (Page 22)
*Sounds of a busy railway station come up, including
platform announcements/explanations for delayed
trains to and from Chester, from and to a variety of
stations*

ACT II

Cue 6   **Hilary**: "I get the picture."   (Page 23)
*Garbled announcement, followed by clear announcement
as detailed in script on pages 23-24*

Cue 7   All gather their belongings   (Page 33)
*Garbled announcement followed by clear announcement
as detailed in script on page 33*

Cue 8   **Announcer**: " ... still waiting for that ten quid."   (Page 33)
*Sound of a train approaching the platform,
then reaching a crescendo as the Lights fade down*

Cue 9   Black-out   (Page 34)
*Sound of train stopping, then leaving the platform,
then chugging along*

Cue 10   To open SCENE 2   (Page 34)
Sound of train continues

Cue 11	**Maggie**: "... in the circumstances ..." *Train noise fades out as scene continues*	(Page 34)
Cue 12	**Maggie**: "... all the pieces when it falls down." *Train brakes squeal slightly*	(Page 36)
Cue 13	**Andrew** and **Vicky** enter *Noise of the train fades up*	(Page 37)
Cue 14	**Yvonne** and **Hilary** furtively stack Jenga bricks *Train noise fades down*	(Page 38)
Cue 15	**Yvonne**: " ... do you think you're talking to —— " *Loud squeal of brakes followed by sound of* *train chugging along*	(Page 39)
Cue 16	A pensive mood takes over the group *Train chugs away in the background*	(Page 40)
Cue 17	All heads go down and they write *Faint chugging of the train, which comes up to* *fill the stage with noise and reaches a climax*	(Page 41)

ACT III

Cue 18	To open ACT III, SCENE 1 *Traffic noise can be heard*	(Page 42)
Cue 19	**Hilary**: "Oh, here come the taxis." *Sound of taxis pulling up and car doors opening*	(Page 42)
Cue 20	**Hilary**: "... stop moaning, will you." *Sound of car door slamming*	(Page 42)
Cue 21	**Hilary**: "Here's ours." *Sound effect of car pulling up*	(Page 43)
Cue 21	Black-out *Sound of doors slamming and taxi pulling away.* *Silence for a few seconds then suddenly a very* *loud sound effect of marquee festivities to open Scene 2*	(Page 43)
Cue 22	**Aerobics Instructor** blows his/her whistle *Loud dance music snaps up*	(Page 43)

Cue 23	**Voice of Aerobics Instructor**: "... feel free to sing along if you want to ... *"These Boots Were Made for Walking" blares out*	(Page 46)
Cue 24	**Vicky**: "... you little minx, you!!" *Sound of music rises in volume*	(Page 49)
Cue 25	Black-out *Sound effect of crowd increases in volume*	(Page 50)
Cue 26	To open ACT III, SCENE 3 *General hubbub of a crowd*	(Page 50)
Cue 27	Countdown ends *Loud klaxon sounds*	(Page 54)
Cue 28	To open ACT III, SCENE 5 *Loud sound effect of toilets flushing*	(Page 58)
Cue 29	**Siobhan**: "Well — everything!" *Sound of a toilet flushing*	(Page 60)
Cue 30	To open ACT III, SCENE 6 *Noise of crowds of walkers*	(Page 62)
Cue 31	**Ethel/Ron**: " ... well done, well done." *Sounds of the crowd*	(Page 67)
Cue 32	**Handsome Drunk**: "... on the long journey?" *Loud sound effect of fairy dust*	(Page 70)
Cue 33	**Handsome Drunk**: "... make my dream come true?" *Another sound of fairy dust*	(Page 71)
Cue 34	Black-out *Sound of heavy traffic fades up*	(Page 72)
Cue 35	To open ACT III, SCENE 9 *Policeman's whistle sounds*	(Page 72)
Cue 36	**Policeman**: "This is a busy road." *Sound of horn beeping*	(Page 72)
Cue 37	**Policeman**: " ... all be across shortly." *Sound of car screeching away impatiently*	(Page 72)

Cue 38	**Policeman**: "... while we can ..." *Policeman's whistle sounds* *Sound of cars halting*	(Page 73)
Cue 39	**Policeman**: "... all night for you ..." *Sound of traffic starting again*	(Page 73)
Cue 40	**Policeman**: "... that takes the flaming biscuit!" [Original version] *Traffic noises*	(Page 74)
Cue 41	**Policeman**: "Mind that traffic now ..." *Squeals of brakes. Busy traffic noise. Huge squeal* *of brakes and sound of a crash*	(Page 76)
Cue 42	To open ACT III, Scene 10 *"Chariots of Fire" music fades up*	(Page 76)
Cue 43	**All** kiss their medals and wave *Big camera flash and sound effect of crowd cheers*	(Page 76)

ACT IV

Cue 44	To open ACT IV *Sound of busy railway station: a train pulling into* *the station and people emerging and bustling* *down the platforms. Garbled announcement* *fades in and out as detailed in script on p. 77*	(Page 77)
Cue 45	**Maggie** waves off the others *Sound of train departing the station grows* *louder and reaches a crescendo*	(Page 81)
Cue 46	**Maggie** gazes out over the audience **Maggie**'s *pre-recorded voice fades up to echo slowly* *and softly as detailed in the script on p. 82*	(Page 82)
Cue 47	**Maggie's Voice** echoes in the darkness, followed by a slight pause *Music full on*	(Page 82)
Cue 48	**Andrew** takes a photo *Big camera flash*	(Page 82)